THE STORY OF
LONDON'S
UNDERGROUND

John R. Day and John Reed

Historical Consultants: Desmond F. Croome and M.A.C. Horne

Capital Transport

ISBN 978-1-85414-440-9

Published by
Capital Transport Publishing
www.capitaltransport.com

Printed by Parksons Graphics

The coaches, based on the Great Western model but adapted to the narrower gauge, were said to be a great improvement on anything used on the line before and better than many main-line coaches of the era, and the locomotives, designed by Fowler, were certainly better than the rather strange assortment provided by the Great Northern, though these had saved the day for the Metropolitan.

The new locomotives were 4-4-0 tank engines with outside cylinders. The weight, with 1,170 gallons of water in the tanks, was 45 tons. Tractive effort at 80 per cent boiler pressure was 13,100lb. The Fowler locomotives were so successful that they remained, with a few modifications, the motive power of the tunnel lines until electrification. Between them, they eventually numbered 66. When the District came to need its own motive power, it bought engines of the same type from the same builders and this added another 54 to their numbers. One of the 'A' class (No.23) is now preserved by London's Transport Museum. The fuel at first was coke made from the finest Durham coal, but this was superseded after six years by South Wales semi-anthracite coal.

The Metropolitan's own locomotives began to arrive in 1864. No.18 was one of the first batch ('A' type) and is seen in original condition. It carries the name 'Hercules', later removed.

An engraving of Portland Road station viewed from the south side, giving a reasonably accurate impression of its ornate design, but with a rather out-of-scale bus. The two domes on the north side were demolished in 1869/1870 to improve ventilation.

THE ATMOSPHERE OF THE UNDERGROUND RAILWAY.—Sarah Dobner, aged 56, died at the Bishop's-road Station of the Metropolitan Railway on Tuesday before last. Deceased had complained of a great difficulty of breathing while on the underground, and while waiting for the second train she said she was in great pain. A medical gentleman advised her removal to the hospital, but it was then believed she was dead. Mr Anderson, one of the surgeons at St Mary's Hospital, who made the post-mortem examination, said the deceased was labouring under disease of the bronchial gland, and undoubtedly the suffocating air of the Underground Railway had accelerated death. The coroner, at the inquest, said he had experienced the depressing effects of that railway, and he therefore avoided it as much as possible. The tunnels and stations should be ventilated, but he supposed that would not be done until some shocking loss of life from suffocation had occurred. The jury returned a verdict of 'death by natural causes, accelerated by the suffocating atmosphere of the Underground Railway'.

The Builder, 17th August 1867

When the railway started its public service there were outcries about poor ventilation. A fan had to be provided at what was then Portland Road station and glazing was removed above tracks at Baker Street, Portland Road and Gower Street stations. Later, portions of the covered way were opened up to improve ventilation still further, and in 1871–72 'blow-holes' (an idea of Pearson's originally) were made in the tunnel roof to the road above on the section between Edgware Road and King's Cross. The sudden eruption of air, steam, and smoke from these holes as a train passed below was said to have been very disturbing to horses in the roadway above. The ventilation on the railway appears to have been somewhat less than had been promised before the line was built as the station design had been based on the assumption that the fireless locomotive would work properly.

This experience led to stations on extensions and on the District Railway being built as far as possible in the open. There was also, where possible, an intermediate open section between stations. Some of these remain today.

Meanwhile, Fowler had been busy building another railway, the Hammersmith & City. This was built by a separate company with the backing of the Great Western and the Metropolitan and was conceived as a feeder to the Metropolitan line. The new line ran from the Great Western main line about a mile out of Paddington and formed a quarter of a circle round the suburbs of the day to end pointing almost south at Hammersmith. There were intermediate stations at Notting Hill (now Ladbroke Grove) and at Shepherd's Bush (not the present station). A branch left the main line at Latimer Road (the station of that name did not open until 16th December 1868) and ran to Kensington (Addison Road – now Olympia). The main line opened on 13th June 1864 and the branch on 1st July the same year. The 'branch' was in fact a connecting line with the West London and the West London Extension Railway, which gave a route from Paddington via West Brompton and over the Thames to Battersea and the south, including a connection with Victoria. This later resulted in such curiosities as the London, Brighton & South Coast running trains to Brighton from Paddington and broad-gauge Great Western trains working regularly to Victoria (on the London, Chatham & Dover side). The Hammersmith & City became a joint responsibility of the Great Western and Metropolitan on 1st July 1865. The track was mixed gauge. Because of delays to trains on the section of Great Western main line, two extra tracks were put down for the Hammersmith & City, coming into use on 30th October 1871.

So much for the western side of London. Farther east, the Great Northern had started running through trains to Farringdon Street on 1st October 1863, and on the same day the Great Western started running broad-gauge trains between Farringdon and Windsor. In the next month the Metropolitan let the contract for an eastwards extension to Moorgate Street. Powers for this had been obtained in 1861, and the preliminary matters had been taken care of while the earlier part of the line was still being built. The contractor, John Kelk, started work early the next year, but in the meantime a further decision had been made. To keep the Great Northern trains clear of the Metropolitan's and give them proper access to the goods depot and meat market at Smithfield two extra tracks would be laid on the Moorgate extension, and the existing lines would be quadrupled all the way back to King's Cross. This was an undertaking of some magnitude, because it meant building another double-track tunnel at the side of the long Clerkenwell tunnel. The work was authorised in 1864

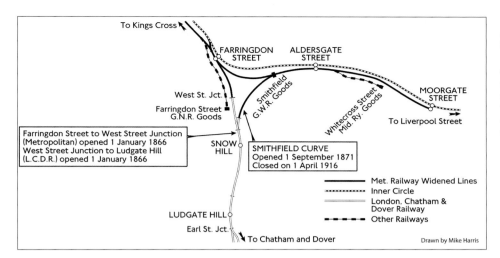

Map of connections from Farringdon Street. The 'Smithfield Curve' opened on 1st September 1871 and closed on 1st April 1916. The connections here were designed to permit the realisation of the Metropolitan Railway's grand vision of through services to the North of England and Kent coast – perhaps even Paris via a Channel Tunnel.

and also went to John Kelk. Fowler, of course, was the engineer. The 'Widened Lines', as they have always been called, run north of the Metropolitan tracks from King's Cross to the 'new' Clerkenwell tunnel. Built between November 1865 and May 1867, the tunnel is 733yds in length. At its eastern end the mouth is some 16ft lower than that of the original tunnel, and the Widened Lines dip under the Metropolitan tracks and run from there to Moorgate on the south side of the other lines. The Metropolitan lines were carried across the Widened Lines by an unusual wrought-iron bridge which also acted at a strut between the walls of the deep cutting. The bridge was well known in railway circles as the 'Ray Street Gridiron'. It was replaced by a concrete raft in 1960, but the girders of the original bridge had already been renewed in 1892/3.

A new station was built at Farringdon Street for the extension, and the line was open from that station for passengers to Moorgate on 23rd December 1865. The Widened Lines were opened for passengers from Farringdon to Aldersgate Street on 1st March 1866 and to Moorgate on 1st July of the same year. The new Clerkenwell tunnel held up the Farringdon–King's Cross opening for passenger traffic until 17th February 1868. Meanwhile, the London, Chatham & Dover had been building towards Ludgate Hill and Snow Hill. This line met a short spur from the Metropolitan at West Street Junction, just south of Farringdon, and a new cross-London route (today used by Thameslink trains) was made available on 1st January 1866. Smithfield market, for the traffic of which so much preparation had been made, was officially opened in November 1868, but not served by trains until 3rd May 1869. A connection had also been made between the newly built Midland Railway line to London and the Metropolitan. This was opened on 13th July 1868 and carried local trains from Bedford into Moorgate. As St Pancras was not to be opened for another 2½ months, Moorgate was in fact the Midland's first London terminus.

The Great Western broad-gauge trains had been projected from Farringdon to Aldersgate and then to Moorgate over the new Widened Lines when they were opened – they were mixed-gauge lines. In August 1868, however, it was agreed that the broad-gauge passenger trains should be withdrawn from the Metropolitan, and the last train on the 7ft gauge left Moorgate on 14th March 1869.

Before we leave this area, it is worth noting that in 1871 a connection from Snow Hill to the Widened Lines in the Moorgate direction was opened – the earlier ones faced King's Cross. London, Chatham & Dover trains reached Moorgate by this route from 1st September 1871, and they continued to use the route until 1st April 1916. The tunnel was demolished in the general clearance of the site of the Smithfield Poultry Market, burnt down in January 1958.

Another Metropolitan move towards expansion, small in itself, was to have much significance later on in the railway's history. In 1864, the Metropolitan & St John's Wood Railway was incorporated, with Fowler as engineer. This was to run from Baker Street to meet the Hampstead Junction Railway near the latter's Finchley Road station. In fact, the line got into financial difficulties and finished up – and then only with the help of the Metropolitan – as a single-track line which left the Met by a junction at Baker Street and ended at Swiss Cottage. It was opened on 13th April 1868. When, in the following year, the St John's Wood proposed to increase its through services over the Metropolitan line to six trains an hour instead of three, the Metropolitan declined. Following two small accidents and other difficulties at the Baker Street junction, the Met closed the junction and refused to allow through trains.

Very few persons who have come underground, say from Edgware Road to King's Cross, about three or four o'clock in the day, will think any language that we can venture to print sufficiently strong to reprobate the intolerable and stifling atmosphere into which those passengers have to descend who seek to shun the fierce sun of the streets, and the intermitting torture of the public conveyances. But now that we have the authority of the coroner for attributing death *directly* to the atmosphere of the Underground Railway, we trust that the directors of that enterprise will feel convinced that it will pay to attend to the ventilation of their pestiferous tunnels. The traffic on the railway is enormous, and, conducted as it is by fully adequate locomotive power, and unimpeded by the delays caused by junctions, or by the charging and uncharging of luggage, it is calculated to relieve the streets almost entirely of a large amount of through traffic, were it not for this one grand obstacle, want of ventilation. There can, we should think, be little doubt that a due attention to this essential requisite of comfort would very largely increase the traffic of the Metropolitan Railway.
The Builder, 24th August 1867

Competition between the District and Metropolitan is well evident in these adverts from the 1880s.

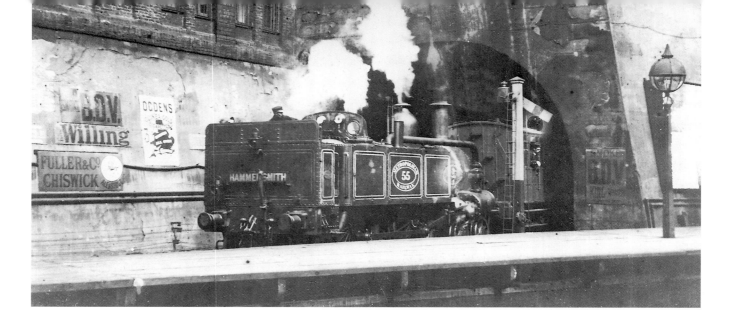

Steaming Ahead

At Aldgate the platforms were very tightly confined within the western side of the triangular junction. This view shows a Hammersmith train (which did not call at Aldgate) emerging from the tunnel from Aldgate East and passing the northern end of the platforms at Aldgate. This loco, a 'B' class built in 1879, is running tender first; locos were not routinely turned at the end of their journeys (though they were turned at intervals to reduce uneven wheel wear occasioned by continuous working around the Inner Circle service).

So far we have seen the Metropolitan under Watkin as a disgruntled parent doing its best to obstruct and control an upstart child, the District, which persisted in kicking over the traces. This is a long way from being the whole picture; probably Watkin considered it not much more than an irritating sideline. He had his mind on bigger things.

It will be recalled that there was a short single-track line, the St John's Wood, running north-west for nearly two miles to Swiss Cottage from a junction with the Metropolitan at Baker Street. This line had double track at the two intermediate stations, St John's Wood and Marlborough Road, and was complete to within a short distance of the North London's Finchley Road station. It had been opened, as already described, on 13th April 1868. The Metropolitan Railway's original route between Paddington and Farringdon was always regarded as the 'main line'. When the St Johns Wood Railway was opened, it instantly became known as 'the extension' in official documents or as 'the Wood Line' amongst the staff.

Sir Edward Watkin had appeared on the Metropolitan scene in 1872, and in 1873 the St John's Wood line obtained powers to extend to Kingsbury (the station now known as Neasden). The reason for this, Watkin explained later, was two-fold. The cramped works at Edgware Road were to be moved out into the country and the Metropolitan was to break through 'the iron barrier which the skill and acuteness of the larger railway companies had constructed' around it. They wanted to cross the Midland and the North Western lines so that, if an extension was called for at any time, it would go to the Metropolitan and not to the others.

Watkin was a main-line man, and he looked on the Metropolitan as a potential main-line railway. In 1874 he asked the shareholders to approve a proposal to carry the St John's Wood line on to Harrow, and he tempted them by speaking of 'disjointed pieces of railway which will hereafter help to connect your great terminus with Northampton and Birmingham and many other important towns.' The shareholders must have had their field of vision suddenly enlarged. They had put their money in a small, busy, London railway; here was the chairman talking in familiar terms of the Midlands.

The extension was put in hand. On 30th June 1879, the St John's Wood line was open to West Hampstead; it was doubled from Baker Street to Swiss Cottage on 10th July 1882, the new track running in a separate tunnel alongside the old. On 24th November 1879 it was opened to Willesden Green and on 2nd August 1880 to Harrow-on-the-Hill, powers having been granted for this in an Act of 1874. The Metropolitan, through its St John's Wood company, had now reached out 9½ miles from Baker Street. Among many proposals for building new links and joining existing lines at this period was one, in which Watkin had a hand, for making a new route from the Midlands which would enter London via the Metropolitan. This plan eventually reached Parliament as the Buckinghamshire & Northamptonshire Railways Union Bill, but it was rejected.

SIR EDWARD WATKIN, BART., M.P
From a Photograph by Walery, Regent Street, W.

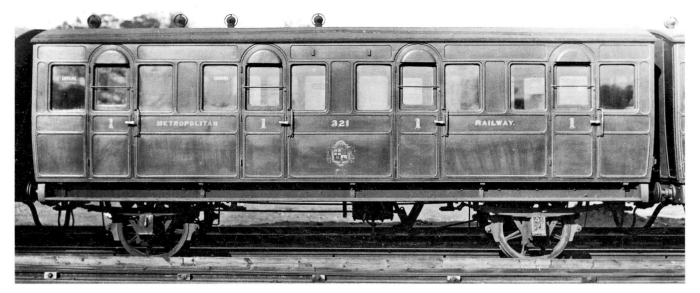

Although the Metropolitan was granted powers in 1880 to build on to Rickmansworth and in the following year to Aylesbury, Pinner was not reached until 25th May 1885 and Rickmansworth on 1st September 1887. The Metropolitan, which by now had taken over the St John's Wood line completely, had its railhead 17½ miles from Baker Street. Meanwhile, in 1886, Watkin was accused at a general meeting of concealing the real reason for this advance to the north-west. Watkin dismissed the implication as a 'phantom of the imagination', having conveniently forgotten his promises of 1874 about the future of the Metropolitan's 'great terminus'.

Nevertheless, although the Metropolitan could not at once raise the money to go on to Aylesbury, it did continue to Chesham. The main line from Rickmansworth to Amersham and north-westwards to Aylesbury was authorised by the Aylesbury & Rickmansworth Railway Act of 1881, and the Chesham branch by the Metropolitan Railway Act of 1885, which empowered the Metropolitan to build a branch railway 2½ miles long from the point where it diverges from the main line, some three-quarters of a mile from Chalfont & Latimer station.

Most of the land for the new sections of railway was purchased at the time from the Duke of Bedford and Lord Chesham, but the land for the final half-mile of the Chesham branch was presented to the railway by the inhabitants to ensure that a station could be built in the centre of Chesham instead of on the outskirts, as was originally intended. The Metropolitan subsequently purchased further strips of land extending almost 1½ miles north of the station in the direction of Berkhamsted, land it never used.

In May 1889 the double-track railway from Rickmansworth through Chorleywood to Chalfont Road (as Chalfont & Latimer station was known until November 1915) and the single-track branch to Chesham were almost complete; so, in recognition of their generosity, the people of Chesham were invited to a ceremonial opening on 15th May and were entertained to a banquet. Seven weeks later, on 8th July, the line from Rickmansworth to Chesham was opened to public traffic. The main line

Metropolitan 4–wheeled compartment carriage No. 321, built in 1889 (Jubilee stock) and one of the 27 carriages modernised in 1908–1909 and fitted with electric lighting. There are roof ventilators above the smoking compartments only. Nine-coach trains of this stock were hauled by electric locomotives but withdrawn from Metropolitan service in 1912.

Chesham terminus on the official opening day, 15th May 1889.

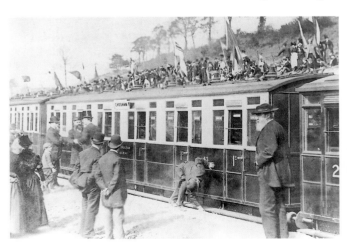

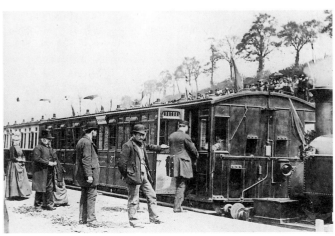

The terminus at the City end was at the junction of King William Street and Arthur Street (now Monument Street); the station building itself was No.46 King William Street. In those days the tubes, like the sub-surface lines, found it expedient to avoid legal arguments and compensation by following the line of the streets above. This meant that the City terminus had to be built to run roughly east and west and that the line had to curve round just after leaving the station to pass under the river (see map). It ran under Arthur Street, which was so narrow that the two tunnels had to run one above the other to keep beneath the street itself, and then under Swan Lane, at the end of which stood Old Swan Pier. South of the river, the line was to pass under Borough High Street and Newington Causeway to the Elephant, a total distance of 1½ miles. Intermediate stations were to be built at Denman Street (London Bridge) and Great Dover Street (Borough).

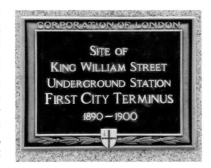

Commemorative plaque at the site of the original City terminus of the first deep level tube railway.

In February 1886 the main contract for the tunnels and stations was placed with Edmund Gabbutt, a Liverpool contractor. Preparations began in May, and work started in October from a shaft sunk from a temporary staging behind the Old Swan Pier. From this shaft the driving of the upper (up line) tunnel southwards began the same month. The lower (down) tunnel was not started until the following March, and then it was driven so that it rose to the same level as the up tunnel, and to the west of it, on the south side of the river. These tunnels were 10ft 2in in diameter and accommodated a standard-gauge railway track.

In 1887 powers were obtained to continue the line southwards to Stockwell, making the line just over three miles in length. It was decided that the tunnels on this section should be 10ft 6in in diameter because the gradients were easier and the trains could be run at a higher speed. The engine house to be built at the Elephant would drive one cable for the City section at 10mph and another for the Stockwell section at 12mph. The contract for the new section of the line was let to Walter Scott & Company, of Newcastle, the same firm also completing the City section when ill-health caused Edmund Gabbutt to withdraw.

Contracts for the lifts had been placed, and so had those for the cable apparatus, but doubts began to be expressed about the wisdom of cable working. Electric traction had already been mooted for other lines, as we have seen, and what really seems to have turned the scales was the success of the electrically-operated Bessbook & Newry Railway in Ireland, opened in 1885. That electric traction was practicable had already been shown in Great Britain, for Magnus Volk had opened his electric railway at Brighton in 1883.

The technical press was already drawing the attention of the chairman of the City of London & Southwark, Charles Grey Mott, to the advantages of electric traction, and he sought professional advice. In its report for the half-year in August 1888, the board told the shareholders that experiments were to be made with electric traction pending a decision on its use. One of the most famous signal engineers of the day, C.E. Spagnoletti, who has already been mentioned in connection with the signalling of the Metropolitan Railway, was called in as consultant on electric traction. This caused some comment at the time, as he had had no experience in this field, but there is no reason to doubt that his advice was sound.

In January 1889 a contract was placed with Mather & Platt Ltd, who undertook to supply the power necessary to run a three-minute service from each station and to run the trains at a higher average speed than those of the Inner Circle. They also gave a guaranteed cost per train-mile for a period of two years – lower than the cost of steam working if steam working had been allowed. An experimental train was to be provided by the contractors.

Meanwhile, work proceeded on the stations and tunnels. The King William Street terminus site was reached by a shaft from above, but eventually most of the debris from the station works and the City end of the tunnels went out by the shaft in the river at Old Swan Pier. When the work was completed, this shaft was sealed and made watertight over the tunnels and the staging was removed. At platform

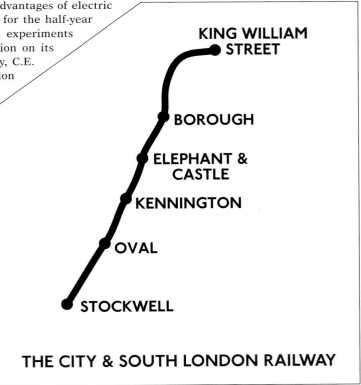

KING WILLIAM STREET

BOROUGH

ELEPHANT & CASTLE

KENNINGTON

OVAL

STOCKWELL

THE CITY & SOUTH LONDON RAILWAY

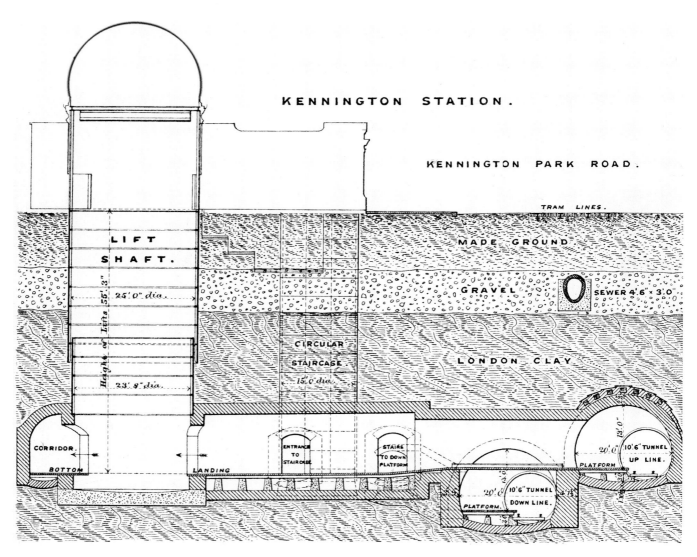

KENNINGTON STATION.

KENNINGTON PARK ROAD.

Cross section of Kennington station as originally built. The station tunnels had a 3ft deep brick lining, and the terminal stations had tunnels 26ft wide and 20ft high. At intermediate stations there were tunnels for each line, each tunnel being 20ft wide, 16ft high (13ft from platform level), and 200ft long. Stockwell terminus differed from the layout shown and had an island platform with a track on each side. The reason for the different heights of platforms at intermediate stations was to reduce the number of steps between platform and lift landing. This was achieved completely at Oval, with low-level inclines to both platforms.

level the station had a single track with a platform on each side – a design suitable for cable operation but not electric. The street was reached by two hydraulic lifts running in a single 25ft diameter shaft. The gas-lit station was modified in 1895 (while still operational!) and became a two-track layout with an island platform between the two tracks. At the Stockwell end a 1-in-3½ incline led from the station to the rolling stock depot at the side of Spurgeon's Orphanage in the Clapham Road. Cable haulage was needed to take stock up this incline. The intermediate stations were Borough, Elephant & Castle, Kennington, and Oval.

Experimental running began in September 1889 with one locomotive and two coaches. The track was not yet complete, nor was the generating station at Stockwell, so current was taken, on the three-rail system, from a temporary generating station at the Borough, from which point the rails to the City were complete. The first tunnel went through to Stockwell in January 1890, and a second, geared, locomotive arrived for trials in February. On 7th March the company felt sufficiently confident of progress to take the Lord Mayor and other guests from the City to the Elephant. They also proposed to take them back again to a special luncheon, but the water company, having found some defect, turned off the supply of water to the temporary generating plant, which had to be hastily shut down. The party did get back by rail, an hour late, but the effect on the food – and tempers – is not known. Everyone had recovered enough to take Metropolitan Railway directors on a similar trip the following week.

The formal opening was on 4th November 1890; it was performed by the Prince of Wales (later King Edward VII). In the meantime, the company's name had been changed to the City & South London Railway to match its enlarged status – still further enlarged by the granting of Parliamentary authority to continue the line to Clapham – and it was under this name that the line was opened. The party travelled

The City & South London construction site at Stockwell where, as at many other locations, property had to be demolished to make space for work and for the later erection of a surface station.

from King William Street to Oval to look at the works and equipment, and then on to Stockwell for lunch in a marquee in the rolling-stock depot. The general manager had been appointed – T.C. Jenkin, a former London, Tilbury & Southend Railway accountant – and so had the resident engineer, who was Basil (later Sir Basil) Mott. Pleased as they no doubt were with the ceremony and the electric locomotive specially painted for the occasion in cream and grey and named Princess of Wales, they were

The Prince of Wales arriving at Stockwell station after formally opening the railway – 4th November 1890. The party was walking towards the lifts.

TAKING THE TICKET AT BANK STATION.

No worry about price
2ª any distance

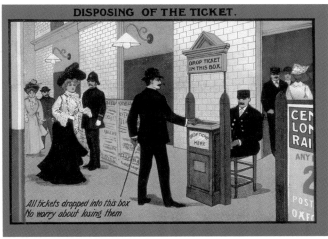

DISPOSING OF THE TICKET.

All tickets dropped into this box
No worry about losing them

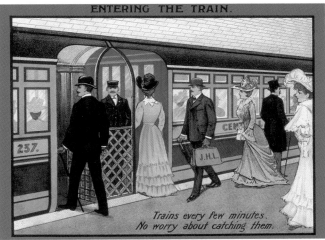

ENTERING THE TRAIN.

Trains every few minutes.
No worry about catching them.

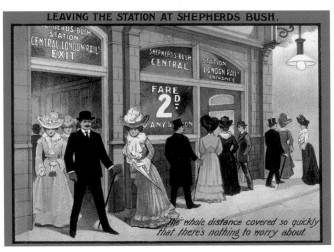

LEAVING THE STATION AT SHEPHERDS BUSH.

The whole distance covered so quickly
that there's nothing to worry about.

With its flat fare of 2d and its careful siting to tap a main traffic stream, the Central London proved the potential of tube railway travel. It was the first really modern tube. Its smart trains, hauled by their electric locomotives in crimson lake with gold lining and polished brass-work, opened the eyes of London to the possibilities of underground travel far more than the CSLR or the Waterloo & City had done. In the five remaining months of 1900 it carried nearly 15 million passengers, running from 5am to midnight on weekdays, with a reduced service on Sundays. The route, connecting the residential areas of west London with the City and running the length of Oxford Street to serve the shopping and theatre areas, could scarcely have been better chosen to attract passengers at all times of the day and evening.

It was not long, however, before the Central London ran into trouble. The attractive American-built double-bogie locomotives, with their central cabs, had their armatures built directly on to the axles, obviating gears and making them very quiet. Their four motors gave them 800hp (one-hour rating) and a tractive effort at starting of 14,100lb. Efficient as the system of mounting the motors was, it meant that of the locomotive weight of 44 tons only a quarter was spring-borne, and they set up a vibration which disturbed property owners along the line so much that a Board of Trade committee was set up to investigate.

The Central London Railway co-operated whole-heartedly in the enquiry, which confirmed that there was serious vibration, and three of its locomotives were converted to operate with 150hp geared motors. This reduced the weight to 31 tons, of which 21 tons were spring-borne. The railway also made up two six-car trains with two cars in each train converted to motor cars by fitting them with two 100hp geared motors each, giving 400hp per train. Tests with the geared locomotives showed that the vibration was greatly reduced, but no vibration was noticed at any point on the surface when the multiple-unit trains ran below. As a result of these trials the railway decided to replace the locomotives by 64 motor cars to form multiple-unit trains of seven cars, although six-car trains soon became the norm. A new motor giving 125hp was designed

These four pictures have been extracted from a larger poster, and show how easy it is to buy a ticket, surrender it on entry, board a train and leave the destination station. The words at the foot of each picture are all on the theme of 'no worry', respectively about price, losing your ticket, catching your train (because the service is so frequent) and taking a long time for your journey. The Central London originally intended to follow the main line tradition of providing some first class carriages. A number of cars were supplied with floral patterned seating to that end but, when they entered service, all cars were the same class.

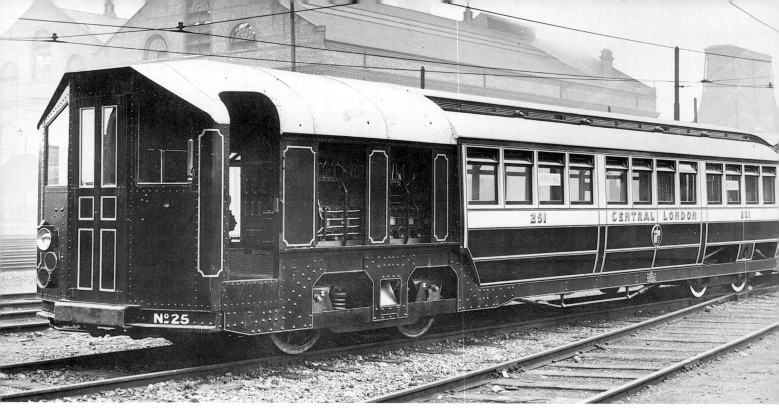

Above Driving motor car 251 of multiple unit train No. 25 of 1903 is seen at Wood Lane depot when new, one of a fleet of 64 new vehicles that replaced the original electric locomotives after only three years of use. Overhead wiring was installed at the depot so that the remaining locos could haul the stock around the unelectrified track.

Below right A painting of one of the new multiple-unit trains. The direction sign to the C&SLR tells us that the station is the Bank terminus.

At first the CLR trains were very labour-intensive, and eight men were carried on a seven-car train: the driver and his assistant, a front and rear guard, and four gatemen. Starting the train was a complicated ritual, with each gateman facing the front of the train and holding up his hand when the gates were shut. When the front guard saw the correct number of hands he showed a green light to the rear, to which the rear guard responded by showing a green light forward and blowing a whistle. On receiving these signals the front guard showed a green light forward to the driver or his assistant, and the train could start.

J. Graeme Bruce

for the stock, giving 500hp per train. The service was being fully worked with the new trains by June 1903. The easier turn-round made a two-minute service possible against the 2½ minute service which was the best that could be provided with the locomotives. At first, the motor cars had to be manned by a crew of two, but later, after the adoption of the 'dead man's handle', only a driver was required.

An interesting feature of the locomotives was that they had a series-parallel controller of the drum type made up of a wooden cylinder with the copper segments attached. This drum was of no less than 18in diameter and required some physical effort to move it. To assist him with a certain amount of leverage, the driver was provided with a control handle 21 inches in length! After replacement by multiple-unit trains, all but two of the locomotives were scrapped. For a time another two locomotives were used by J.S. Raworth, after adaptation, to demonstrate his regenerative braking system on the Metropolitan, but were soon scrapped.

Just before the First World War, the passenger fleet comprised 64 motor cars, 133 trailers and 38 control trailers. Two 0-6-0 steam locomotives were mainly used to shunt trailer cars in the depot yard but also when power was off in the tunnels. Built to tube loading gauge by the Hunslet Engine Co. Ltd in 1899, these were side-tank locomotives fitted with condensing apparatus. They were oil-fired in the tunnels but coal could be burnt in the open, and a small coal bunker was provided for the purpose. They were sold in 1920 and 1921. The last of the two retained electric locomotives was in service for shunting purposes until 1942.

Interior of a 1900 trailer car, with leather-covered armrests and rattan-covered seats. Some cars had moquette upholstery.

In 1902 a Bill was submitted to Parliament for powers to extend the line from Shepherd's Bush to Hammersmith, Piccadilly, Strand, and the City to form a 'Central London Circle', on which it was proposed to operate a service similar to that provided by the Circle line. The Bill was rejected, and although revived in 1903 and 1905, was eventually abandoned; the opening in 1906 of the Great Northern, Piccadilly & Brompton Railway from Hammersmith to Finsbury Park (now part of the Piccadilly Line) had removed many of the original attractions of the scheme.

The Central London Railway carried on with its flat fare of 2d for several years but traffic began to decline from its peak of about 44.9 million in 1904 giving rise to some concern; by 1907 it had dropped by nearly 18 per cent. The initial response was to increase fares to 3d for the longer distance journeys (more than 7 or 8 stations) from 1st July. The following year traffic picked up, mainly due to the extra loadings serving the Franco-British exhibition that opened on 14th May 1908 adjacent to a new Central London station at Wood Lane; even so, there was no room for complacency as numbers fell again when the exhibition closed at the end of October. The feeling was that for comparatively short journeys the railway fared badly against the buses running directly above where fares were only a penny and, when the times taken to get to and from platforms were taken into account, could often be quicker for short distances, especially when buses then stopped anywhere on request. Perhaps of most significance was that horse buses were being replaced rapidly by faster and larger motor buses; there were just 20 motors in 1905 and nearly 800 at the start of 1907. In response, fares for just three stations were reduced to a penny from 5th March 1909. This appeared to have helped arrest decline and 1909 carryings were just over 38 million.

The Central London's signalling was mechanical and very much like that on the City & South London, using Spagnoletti's lock-and-block system. There were semaphore starting signals at the platforms, but in the tunnels, where there was less room, the inner and outer home signals were sliding coloured spectacles. Between the Bank and Shepherd's Bush there were 14 signalboxes. These included separate boxes for each direction at the three two-level stations – Post Office, Chancery Lane, and Notting Hill Gate. As on the CSLR, the block section extended from the starting signal at one station to the outer home of the next, the line between the outer home and the starting signal at that station forming a separate section controlled by the signalman at the station concerned. The brush-on-last-bogie system was employed to check that a train had actually passed inside the outer home. There were signalboxes at each terminal station in addition to the 14 mentioned. Track circuits and automatic signals were installed eventually, the work beginning in 1912.

in May 1909 by a new station on the main line, so that trains no longer had to reverse. (Northfields station had opened as Northfield Halt the year before.) The line from Hounslow Town (renamed Hounslow East in 1925) to Hounslow Barracks (renamed Hounslow West) was single-track for some time with one intermediate station called Heston Hounslow (now Hounslow Central). The single-track was doubled on 1st November 1912 to Heston Hounslow and to Hounslow West on 27th November 1926.

The trains bought for the District's new mainline electric service had powered doors, controlled by a 'gateman' stationed between the cars. Each door was opened and closed by an air cylinder mounted at the top, but the closing action was too powerful, causing injuries and damaging the very full Edwardian clothing worn in those days. The system was also very unreliable and was withdrawn in 1908 so that doors became passenger-operated. The idea was ahead of its time. Air-operated doors were introduced on the Piccadilly Line in 1921, using a different system, and then gradually spread over the whole network. The last hand-worked doors were removed from the District in 1960.

The greater part of the District's new stock, however, was of American design and comprised seven-car trains of three motor cars and four trailers each. All cars were 49ft 6½in over body ends, 8ft 10½in wide and 12ft 3¼in high from rail level. It was open saloon stock, the two end motor cars and the intermediate motor car seating 48, trailer cars 52 and end motor cars with a luggage compartment 40. The general plan was the same as that used for the cars of the Brooklyn Elevated. All the main electrical equipment was British but the cars were built partly by British builders and partly on the Continent.

A four-car train of B-stock in Ealing Broadway station in 1908. The Non Stop disc on the front would have alerted passengers to check which stations the trip would be passing. There was a confusing range of combinations and the number of stations 'Non Stopped' varied between one and seven.

Two of the ten District electric locomotives which entered service in 1905 to haul London & North Western trains between Earl's Court and Mansion House, and were later used to haul Southend-on-Sea trains between Ealing and Barking.

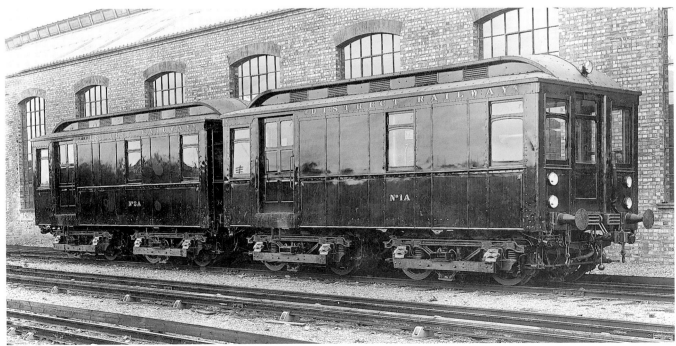

New Tubes

We left the Yerkes forces about to build the Brompton & Piccadilly Circus, the Charing Cross, Euston & Hampstead, the Baker Street & Waterloo, and the Great Northern & Strand. Of these, the Baker Street & Waterloo was the first to be started and the first to be opened. It owed its inception, it is said, to a semi-humorous suggestion by some Westminster businessmen that they should have such a line to take them to Lord's as quickly as possible. Examined in a more serious mood, the scheme proved to have merits.

A Bill was promoted in 1891 and came before a Joint Committee of both Houses in 1892. It became an Act in 1893, and work started in 1898. In 1899 the company promoted a Bill for two extensions – to Paddington, and to Euston as well as a deviation in Lambeth. The two northern extensions in this Bill failed, but another was introduced in 1900 and secured authorisation for the extensions to the Elephant & Castle and to Paddington.

Work started in June 1898 with the erection of a staging in the Thames close to Hungerford Bridge. On this was built a small village of workshops and offices, as well as a power station to give power and light for construction work. From this staging two vertical shafts were sunk into the bed of the river so that excavated material could be taken away by barge. It was also intended to take working material in by the same route. The northbound tunnel was started from this point in February 1899, and the shield began to eat its way slowly – 8 feet per day – towards Trafalgar Square, reaching the station site there in November. By then the southbound tunnel had been started and some of the station work had been put in hand, including Piccadilly Circus and Baker Street. The stations were to be, from the south (including some later authorisations), Elephant & Castle, Kennington Road, Waterloo, Thames Embankment, Trafalgar Square, Piccadilly Circus, Oxford Circus, Regent's Park, Baker Street, Lisson Grove, Edgware Road, and Paddington.

As the railway itself put it in the brochure issued to celebrate its opening, 'the advantages which this line will afford for getting quickly and cheaply from one point of London to another are without parallel. It will link up many of the most important Railway termini, give a connection with twelve other Railway systems, and connect with the vast tramway system of the south of London, thus bringing the theatres and other places of amusement, as well as the chief shopping centre, within easy reach of outer London and the suburbs'. But this was in the future, and misfortune was to befall the line before that. In 1900 came the Whitaker Wright financial failure, and with it the collapse of the Baker Street & Waterloo's backers, the London & Globe Finance Corporation. Work on the line slowly came to a stop and the sites remained derelict for some months until Yerkes came along and bought up the remains.

With Yerkes behind it, work started again in 1902 and tunnelling reached a speed of up to 73 feet a week. The same year the Brompton & Piccadilly Circus and the Great Northern & Strand companies were merged as the Great Northern, Piccadilly & Brompton Railway. Similar merging of the Bakerloo and Hampstead railways was proposed in 1903 but these were not merged in the Great Northern, Piccadilly & Brompton until 1910, and the composite company thus formed was named the London Electric Railway. By such means the tube companies were able to further their integration to mutual benefit.

Meanwhile work on the Baker Street & Waterloo continued. One new practice adopted was to fill the lower part of the tubes with concrete on which the sleepers could rest, the ends of the sleepers being embedded in crushed granite. This helped to reduce vibration, but was adversely criticised in the technical press and was not perpetuated. Because the rails had to go down the shafts driven into the river bed they had to be kept short, and no rail on the original line was longer than 36ft 5in. A four-rail system was used, but it was discovered that there was a leakage to earth from the outside positive rail, which was near the cast-iron tunnel lining. This caused difficulties at the large Charing Cross substation, which fed the District tracks as well as those of the Bakerloo, and the solution adopted was to change the polarity of the rails so that the centre rail became positive instead of negative. This change remained until 1917, when the Bakerloo went out to Watford and it was desirable to standardise the current supply. By this time advances in technique had made it possible to overcome the original difficulties.

The 'straphanger' as seen in this 1912 poster is a term of American origin and is known as early as 1893. It relates to those members of the travelling public who, unable to obtain a seat, held onto the flexible straps or hangers, and who swayed gently to and fro according to the movement of the vehicle. Straps were common in railway and tramway vehicles of open plan design and allowed a significant extra load to be carried; sometimes the extra load got out hand but it was the great Yerkes who swept objection about his overcrowded Chicago trams aside with the retort that 'it is the straphanger who pays the dividend'. Leather straps were provided on all of London Underground's saloon stock from the early days of electrification. These gave way in the mid 1930s to a ball-shaped device on a flexible rubber stalk. These were found to be too easy to detach, making a handy cosh. An improved design emerged in 1943 with a reinforcing chain and external protective spring, and this design was used on all subsequent Underground stock until 1983. On later stock, and on refurbished stock, the hand grips were replaced by simple grab rails. People do of course still stand, rigidly clutching one of the rails provided, but it is now an artless activity and gone is the gentle formation swaying that characterised a true straphanger.

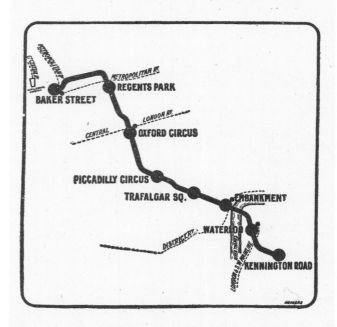
This double sided leaflet was issued shortly after the opening of the Baker Street & Waterloo Railway in March 1906 and shows that the Bakerloo nickname, given to it by the Evening News, was officially adopted very quickly. Kennington Road station was renamed Lambeth North within a few months of opening and Elephant & Castle was opened in August. Passenger numbers would have been much lower than today, which – coupled with draughty trains – probably explains the claim made for a maximum temperature of 60 degrees. Passenger numbers were also much lower than had been hoped; in commercial terms it was the most disappointing of the early tubes. Like all the tube railways that preceded it, the Bakerloo began life with a flat fare of 2d, though this did not last long. The City & South London Railway had abandoned its 2d flat fare when the Moorgate extension opened in February 1900. The Bakerloo moved from a flat fare on 22nd July 1906 and the Central London Railway began charging 3d for longer journeys from the end of June 1907.

Overleaf The original tiling scheme at Oxford Circus Bakerloo station as drawn by Doug Rose.

Automatic signalling with train stops was provided from the start, and there were bare telephone wires along the tunnels. The risk of fire, said the company, was practically non-existent. "The Station Platforms are constructed of concrete and iron, and the Permanent way sleepers of Jarrah, an Australian wood which is non-combustible. The Rolling Stock is built almost entirely of steel, the small quantity of wood used being rendered nonflammable. 'There is a lighted footway from end to end of the line. Special Electric Lamps are placed in the tunnels at intervals of 40 feet. The wires for lighting these lamps are entirely independent of the power cables. The space between the rails has been filled in with cement and granite chippings. Should a train come to a standstill and be unable to proceed, the power current would be at once cut off, and passengers would only have to walk a few hundred yards along an easy and well-lighted footpath to the nearest station.'

The lifts had exit gates opened and shut by compressed air, and passengers entered them at one side and left them at the other. The entrance gates were hand-worked. The stations were decorated in different colour schemes at platform level, the idea being that a passenger could recognise his own station by the colour scheme peculiar to it. Externally, the stations were all similar in pattern. They were designed by Leslie W. Green in the form of a plinth, the idea being that more storeys could be added above this base later on. They were given strength by a steel frame and were faced with glazed blocks in a ruby-red shade. There were no surface buildings on the Bakerloo at Regent's Park, Trafalgar Square or Embankment.

The multiple-unit rolling stock was, as already mentioned, nearly all-steel in its construction. It was built in the USA by the American Car & Foundry Company and sent over in sections for erection in Britain. There were 36 motor-cars and 72 trailers formed into three-car sets which could run in six-car trains in peak hours and as three-car trains at others. The cars had end platforms with gates and carried attendants, who were responsible for working the gates at the ends of adjacent cars and calling out the station names. A guard (or conductor) travelled in the first car. He was also trained as a driver (motorman) and was expected to take over if the regular driver became incapacitated for any reason. The conductor had to join the attendants in calling out the station names. The rolling stock depot and repair shops were in an open three-acre site at St George's Circus, Lambeth, near the southern end of the line.

It was the Central London Railway and its architect Harry Bell Measures who introduced terracotta construction to the tube, though Leslie Green is the one remembered for his glazed terracotta buildings that went up six years later. In terms of architectural design, Measures was mainly influenced by a style nicknamed 'Pont Street Dutch'. As the name suggests, this was a style of building inspired by Flemish Renaissance examples used in speculative developments around Pont Street, Belgravia, and South Kensington and Chelsea in the 1870s. Exponents of the style included Norman Shaw and J. J. Stevenson, and it was used to suggest ostentation in a style alternative to the Gothic or Elizabethan. Measures sought to distinguish the CLR stations by basing them on upmarket London residential architecture of the period, adapted to the mass-manufacture methods available to producers of the unglazed terracotta he chose to use.

The American influence on early Underground train design has already been mentioned. Here is one of the original Hampstead Tube trains at Golders Green, showing also some influence from the USA. It is on a fast service that omitted a number of stations between this point and central London.

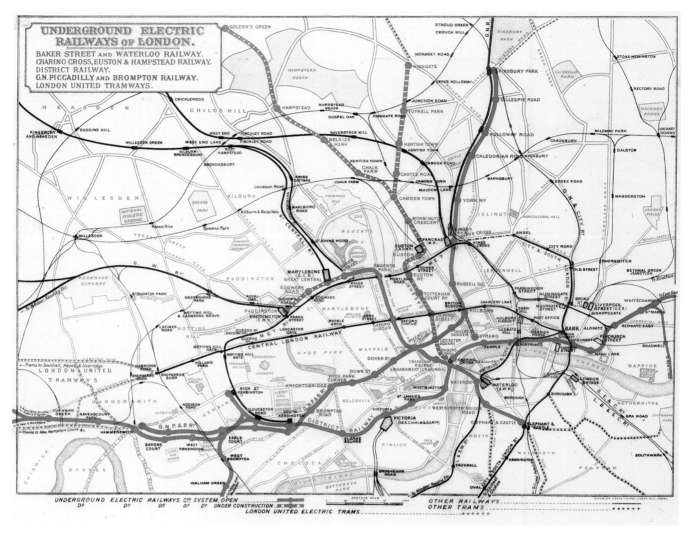

UNDERGROUND ELECTRIC RAILWAYS OF LONDON.
BAKER STREET AND WATERLOO RAILWAY.
CHARING CROSS, EUSTON & HAMPSTEAD RAILWAY.
DISTRICT RAILWAY.
G.N. PICCADILLY AND BROMPTON RAILWAY.
LONDON UNITED TRAMWAYS.

UNDERGROUND ELECTRIC RAILWAYS Cº SYSTEM, OPEN
Dº   Dº   Dº   Dº   Dº UNDER CONSTRUCTION
LONDON UNITED ELECTRIC TRAMS
OTHER RAILWAYS
OTHER TRAMS

The beginnings of a combined Underground map, 1907.
The Underground Electric Railways of London Ltd (UERL) published this map following the opening of the Great Northern, Piccadilly & Brompton Railway in December 1906. Lines outside the group – the Met, the Central London and the CSLR – are shown by thin black lines in common with non-UERL railways. With minor penetration of the Underground into south London – a consequence of the poor soil conditions south of the Thames for tube tunnelling – very little of south London appears on the map.

A busy scene at Bank station, City & South London Railway, c.1910, with the original type of locomotive, as seen in the illustrations earlier, and Brush built cars of 1906/07.

After a major fire on the Paris Underground in 1903 the Board of Trade made strict regulations about the employment of fire-proof materials, and these were applied to the new lines opened after 1904, but there was no imperative for the older railways to comply. A serious fire on the City & South London Railway at Moorgate in July 1908 (and a second fire that year on that company's line) caused a public outcry, magnified by a major conflagration the same year on a Liverpool–Southport electric train which showed just how much destruction was possible. The Board of Trade made several recommendations including the removal of wood at stations underground. All this made the position of pre-1904 tube railways untenable; a programme of enhanced fire protection was followed which brought them close to compliance with the 1904 regulations. In particular the enhanced protection of electrical equipment and removal where possible of underground wooden structures, including wooden platforms, very significantly reduced the fire risk. At the same time a more uniform fire protection regime was adopted for all tube lines including (with some resistance from the operators) fire authority inspection.

After a burst of activity in the first decade of the 20th Century, the first tube extension for four years opened on 28th July 1912. This was the section of the Central London Railway between Bank and Liverpool Street, opened six months before the line became part of the Underground Group. The new station at Liverpool Street was the first Underground station to have escalators from the start. It also boasted improved lighting using lamps with wire filaments that consumed one-quarter of the electricity of the carbon filament lamps used previously and gave lighting that was claimed to be 'the nearest approach to daylight of any incandescent electric lamp on the market'.

A crude early use of the Underground branding on the subway at King's Cross, again with the City & South London Railway shown as a separate service.

Platform and escalator at the new Liverpool Street station of the Central London Railway, opened in 1912. By this time wooden platforms were banned for underground stations but the use of wood in escalators was still felt acceptable. The lighting seen on the escalator was the first of its type installed anywhere in Great Britain. Looking remarkably like fluorescent lighting (not invented until 1935), the frosted glass tubing in fact contained a series of small filament lamps spaced and diffused to give a strip light all the way down. Neon tubular lighting had first been demonstrated at an exhibition in Paris in 1910 but could only produce coloured light.

in various diameters (10ft 2ins, 10ft 6ins and 11ft 6ins) were to be enlarged to the LER standard of 11ft 8ins. Under powers granted in 1913 the line was also to be joined to the Hampstead at Camden Town. Powers were already in place to extend the Hampstead from Golders Green to Edgware. Work on both projects began during June 1922. The original intention was to keep much of the CSLR open while work proceeded, although the section from Moorgate Street to Euston was closed temporarily from the night of 8th August, and one station, City Road between Old Street and Angel, was closed permanently. A shield, that allowed trains to pass through it, was specially designed for the tunnel excavation work. A working site was set up at Borough station, which was also closed for the duration. Later Kennington was used as a work site too. On 27th November 1923 there was serious subsidence near Borough station and the line was closed completely until the works finished later the following year. Thus was the unceremonial passing of the original City & South London Railway, with most of its locomotives going for scrap. Many of the wooden carriages found new leases of life as summer houses or workmen's huts.

Two new stations, North Acton and West Acton, opened on the Central London on 5th November 1923. North Acton and West Acton were simple affairs. They were built and owned by the GWR and North Acton offered an interchange with GWR local services. However, the main event in November was saved for Monday the 19th when the Hampstead Tube was extended from Golders Green to Hendon Central. Northwards from Golders Green passengers were taken on a ride through rooftops and cuttings and across viaducts to Brent station. From Brent the line continued above ground to Hendon Central. Brent and Hendon Central stations, designed by the Underground's architect Stanley Heaps, had island platforms partly covered by a canopy, and stairways leading down at Brent and up at Hendon Central to the ticket hall and entrance. The ticket halls at both stations were spacious and stylish. Walls were clad in white tile edged in black and green. Black and white 'chess board' non-slip floor tiles had been laid, and each had a passimeter ticket booth. These would now be standard for every new, and many existing, ticket halls. The station facades were in a mock Georgian style with doric columns in portland stone. The President of the Board of Trade, and local MP, Sir Philip Lloyd-Graeme, officially opened the new extension. The special train used for the ceremony was composed of air-door stock, the motor-cars being converted gate-stock. The trailers used were brand new, and were part of the first delivery of the order for 191 cars for the CSLR modernisation and the Hampstead extension.

From the earliest days of the Metropolitan and District Railways separate tickets were issued from every station to each other, and of each conceivable variety. This not only became unmanageable in terms of space required, but it was quite incompatible with the mounting need to issue tickets ever faster. In the 1920s the process was simplified by grouping all destinations where fares were the same, and this opened the door to widespread issue of tickets by machines, both in ticket offices and by passenger automatic machines. This system lasted until 1948, from when tickets showed just the station of boarding and fare paid. In December 1921 the first automatic ticket machines and 'passimeter' booking office was introduced at Kilburn Park station. The booking clerk in the passimeter booth, which included a gate, issued, dated and cancelled a ticket before releasing the metered gate to admit the passenger. This rather ugly design was replaced by the polished wood version pictured on the poster on the facing page, though there were variations on the theme and further improvements in appearance. Passimeter booths were eventually to appear at most stations on the system, and only finally disappeared when ticket issuing went fully automatic at the end of the 1980s. A few stations, including Sudbury Town, have preserved examples in situ.

New motor-cars for the CLR Ealing
extension on delivery from the Brush
factory in 1915. It was to be five years
before they entered service on the
Central London and they were on loan to
the Bakerloo between 1917 and 1920,
as already mentioned. These were the
first all-enclosed tube cars, swing doors
replacing end gates.

The Coburg Court Hotel harmonises well
with the Central London Railway station
at Queens Road (now Queensway),
which like most tube stations spent its
early life as a single-storey structure
awaiting such development. Also added
since the station was built are the
public telephones in this 1914 view.

The Central London Railway extension to Ealing must have had difficulties in attracting the passenger numbers hoped for. On 1st May 1922 its fares to and from Ealing Broadway were reduced. For example, the fare to Oxford Circus came down 24% from 10½d to 8d (still a far cry from the Twopenny Tube of 20 years earlier). The reason given was to avoid anomalies with District Railway fares to central London and mirrored the situation early in the CLR's life when the Metropolitan had had to reduce its fares in the central area to compete following an 8½ per cent fall in passengers in the three years from the CLR's opening.

The District Railway was included in early 1920s plans for expansion of the network. A southerly extension from Wimbledon was proposed over London & South Western Railway tracks to South Morden and Sutton. It appeared on a New Works map that was published at the end of 1922, but work never started on the extension.

A programme which was to continue and accelerate throughout the 1920s and 1930s was the replacement of lifts by escalators at suitable locations. During 1924 escalators were installed at many stations, including Bank (7th May), Shepherd's Bush (5th November), and at many of the rebuilt CSLR stations: Moorgate Street on 3rd July, and at Stockwell, Clapham North and Clapham Common on 1st December, the day the southern section of the rebuilt line was opened. The Clapham Common machine is noteworthy in that it was the first escalator fitted with cleated steps and comb plates, thereby enabling passengers to walk straight on and off it at each landing, rather than at an angle. At some stations the installation of escalators was still not complete so lifts continued to be used for a while. Higher-speed lifts were installed at Angel. One station with lifts which was not to benefit from escalators was South Kentish Town, which closed on 5th June 1924 because of a power shortage resulting from a strike at the Lots Road power station. It had been little used and never reopened. At Oxford Circus, where a new ticket hall had been built beneath Argyll Street, new escalators to the CLR platforms were brought in on 30th June 1925. Escalators to the Bakerloo platforms had been in use since May 1914. Other stations to benefit from moving staircases included Old Street on 19th August 1925 and Tottenham Court Road from 20th September, a month after the opening of a new ticket hall. Faster lifts were installed at Leicester Square in 1925 and at Holborn the following year. Escalators replaced these at both stations within ten years as the general installation of moving stairs wherever possible continued.

Now working on the line for which it had been built, a CLR 1915-built motor car with original gate stock trailers on a trip from Ealing to Wood Lane arrives at East Acton soon after the extension was opened in 1920. The area still retained much of a rural character despite being only six miles from Oxford Circus but work on a new housing estate has begun. GWR ownership of the station is shown in the emblem in the seats.

Overleaf This magnificent image of Bank station shows the west end of the eastbound platform in the late 1920s and shows the sharp platform approach, the single conductor rails and the cross-sleepers that covered a pit between the rails (with walkway planks on one side). Visible under the platform edge is a white-painted shelf to minimise the potential drop a passenger might experience. These were probably installed when the carriages were rebuilt with centre doors, leaving a gap between train and platform edge (these shelves were soon illuminated as a train arrived).

The stations built for the Piccadilly Line extensions were on a grand scale making full use of upward space and daylight. Here at Sudbury Town, uplighters fixed to the ticket hall floors also provide a useful publicity site. The wooden passimeter booking office is preserved, out of use, at this listed station today.

Work on the various new extensions was under way as 1930 came to an end, and continued during 1931. By the end of the year the tunnelling was complete. Even before the new services started some rebuilt stations were opened including, on 1st March 1931, the new station building at Ealing Common. It was constructed chiefly of granite and portland stone, and its main feature was a heptagonal tower with a wide canopied entrance to the ticket hall. It was situated in the middle of a single-storey building with shop units. A similar new building at Hounslow West opened on 5th July. These stations represented a development of those built for the Morden extension, and were the work of the Underground's chief architect Stanley Heaps in association with Adams, Holden & Pearson. On 6th July a new temporary station opened at Park Royal, adjacent to Western Avenue, and the old Park Royal & Twyford Abbey station was closed.

A couple of weeks later, on 19th July 1931, the new Sudbury Town station opened. It marked the beginning of a new and undoubtedly the most famous era in the development of the Underground station. Sudbury Town was the result of the continued collaboration between Frank Pick and Charles Holden. In the summer of 1930 the two men had made a trip to Europe to see some of the latest architectural developments in Germany, Denmark, Sweden and Holland. It was believed that by planning stations to be functional, laid out with a specific purpose in mind, and with clean lines and shapes, good design would be created by default. The interpretation of this philosophy for the many stations built for the Piccadilly Line extensions was considerably aided by the use of new materials for the basic structures and traditional red brick and glass for much of the surface cladding and finishing. At Sudbury Town everything was cubic and much was symmetrical. The dominant feature, a majestic box-shaped high-elevated tower, containing the entrance and ticket hall, was constructed of red brick and glass, and was reached across a sweeping forecourt. Space constraints were not a consideration here. It was desirable that the station be visible at night, and full effect was made of internal and external illumination. The huge windows in the tower helped considerably, forming a wall of light against the night sky. And it didn't stop with Sudbury Town, because as 1931 progressed work was proceeding on many new Piccadilly Line extension stations in a similar vein.

While the station work was going on, the job of quadrupling the tracks to carry Piccadilly as well as District trains from Hammersmith to Acton Town and Northfields continued. It included the complete rebuilding of Hammersmith station with a frontage in portland stone and new platform canopies and over-bridges in pre-cast concrete. The tracks were completely relocated to serve two new island platforms, with District trains using the outermost tracks. To the west of Hammersmith, new track was laid on a viaduct, which had formed part of the old Southern Railway line from Richmond to Shepherd's Bush. The old platforms at Ravenscourt Park and Turnham Green could still be utilised for District trains, but a new platform was needed at Stamford Brook to serve the eastbound District. West of Turnham Green the embankment had to be built up and widened, and additional road bridges built to widen the line to Acton Town. Chiswick Park station was completely rebuilt, with new platforms to serve District trains, which would use the two outermost of the four tracks. The new station building consisted of a single story entrance with shop units, dominated by a large high-roofed semi-circular glazed ticket hall with a red brick tower on its western side containing the station name and UNDERGROUND bullseye.

There was much preparation for the opening of the first phase of the Piccadilly Line extensions as 1932 gathered pace. From 8th February some of the District local services from Acton Town to Hounslow West and South Harrow were operated by tube stock. The following week, from 14th February, alterations were made to the District Line services at the western end whereby the service from South Acton to Hounslow was cut back to Acton Town, henceforth becoming a simple shuttle service. The section from Acton Town to South Acton had been double-track, but now it was reduced to single-track only. In the east, in contrast, the District was set to expand, as the LMS set about quadrupling their tracks so that District Line trains could run on the 7½ miles from Barking, where the electric service had terminated since 1908, to Upminster.

A new station at Northfields was opened on 19th May 1932, replacing the original Northfields & Little Ealing station. It was in the new Holden style, and consisted of a large box-shaped red brick ticket hall with glazed column sections above a single-storey entrance. There were two island platforms accommodating four tracks.

On Monday 4th July 1932 the Piccadilly Line was extended from Hammersmith to South Harrow and the District service from Acton Town to South Harrow withdrawn. Apart from the new station buildings at Ealing Common and Sudbury Town, work was well advanced on new buildings at Alperton and Sudbury Hill. Again the functionalism style was evident with large box-like ticket halls dominating otherwise single-storey structures which included shop units. At Alperton the top ticket hall tower was adjacent to the platform, the platform canopy rising above even that. A small forecourt added a sweeping effect. Glazing was not as prominent as at Sudbury Town. Similarly at Sudbury Hill the tower was the dominant feature. There was no forecourt, but as with Sudbury Town and Alperton, round bulb lamps atop concrete columns stood guard at the perimeter. The glazed part of the tower contained an open bullseye. The platforms were rebuilt in a complementary style with plenty of glazing and a 'stepped' glass canopy over the staircases. Acton Town, which was not completed until 1933, was basically similar, but had a larger tower with three glazed columns and more shop units.

A stylish feature introduced to Underground stations during the inter-war years were the brass uplighters fixed to the escalator panelling and which in turn reflected light down from the ceilings to the escalators. The uplighters were a feature of new and rebuilt stations in the early thirties.

The District Railway's Sudbury Hill station buildings had been perfectly sufficient for the semi-rural community it had opened in 1903 to serve. But the spreading of suburbia and the prospect of a frequent tube train service meant something larger was needed, Holden's new station of 1932 being the result.

The western extensions were followed on Tuesday 19th July by the first part of the northern extension of the Piccadilly, the 4½ miles from Finsbury Park to Arnos Grove. From Finsbury Park the line proceeded in twin tunnels to Manor House where a first taste of Holden's new underground platform style was to be seen. The whole effect was dominated by biscuit coloured wall tiling inset with decorative metal covers to the ventilation ducting. The platform cross-section was not circular in common with earlier tube stations. The walls were slightly curved up to the circular roof arch and the platforms were illuminated by downlighters fixed beneath the roof vault. The journey to the ticket hall was, of course, by escalator, full use being made of bronze uplighter columns. The general style of the platforms and escalator shafts was to be replicated at the other deep-level stations on the extension. The Manor House ticket hall, which was entirely sub-surface, had a low ceiling and contained a new, more rounded, style of passimeter booth. It lay beneath the busy junction of Seven Sisters Road and Green Lanes and subways linked the ticket hall to the street and to special tramway islands. At Turnpike Lane, a large square ticket hall, adjacent to an even larger ventilation tower created a mini station complex with several shop units. There were plenty of windows in the ticket hall making it light and airy.

An atmospheric night time view of Arnos Grove taken soon after the station opened in 1932. Platform roof lighting takes the eye down through the brilliantly lit interior of a new standard stock motor car and up to the rotunda above the station ticket hall, illuminated from the inside and externally floodlit. How marvellous this must have appeared to the new traveller clutching a return ticket to Leicester Square for a night out in the West End. The new station included car parking facilities, which also appeared at other stations on the Piccadilly extensions where space permitted.

telephone communication system, it was deemed feasible to deploy just one guard per train. Trials began in February 1927 with a train fitted with a driver/guard telephone, and a start was made on converting the whole existing air-door fleet for working by one guard per train the following May, completing in autumn 1928.

Metro-Cammell (formerly Metro Carriage) received orders for more standard stock in 1930 as a replacement for the 1915 Watford stock on the Bakerloo. The order consisted of 22 motor-cars, 20 control-trailers and 20 trailers. These were virtually identical to previous builds, except that the motor-cars had no central door pillar. It was found that this could be removed without causing any problems and its absence was of great benefit to passenger flows on and off the trains.

Standard stock design moved up a notch in 1930 with the ordering of six experimental cars from the UCC. They were built to test features planned for incorporation in the new fleet of trains needed for the Piccadilly extensions, including wider sliding doors. UCC did not build the complete replacement fleet for the Piccadilly Line, contrary to what had been envisaged, and the trains (totalling 275 cars) were built elsewhere, 145 of them by Metro-Cammell who went on to become the major supplier of Underground trains to London.

When the District services in the Acton and Hounslow area were revised in February 1932, in preparation for the Piccadilly extensions to Hounslow west and South Harrow, the section to South Acton become a shuttle service. B-class motor-car No.37 was converted to double-cab for use on the shuttle. What made No.37 unusual was that it was the very first driver-only unit on the Underground. The doors were converted to air operation and in this form it ran until May 1941, making it the last B-class motor coach in passenger service.

New trains were delivered for the Upminster extension of the District Line in 1932 and were generally similar to previous batches supplied from 1927. They were still fitted with hand-worked sliding doors rather than the air-operated doors that had been standard on all new tube stock for almost ten years. The only apparent difference was the guard's door, which was now sliding rather than hinged. This interior view shows the partition segregating the enclosed first class compartment from the rest of the car. The practice of labelling certain cars or compartments 'Smoking' has been maintained here after the tube lines had switched to specifying those cars which were 'No Smoking'. The craftsmanship of the staff at UCC's Feltham works is much in evidence. It was the last train order to be built by UCC, which was wound up in 1933 upon the formation of London Transport.

London Transport Takes Over

Cockfosters, the first Underground station opened under the reign of the LPTB, early in its life. The roof above the tracks was to be replicated in the design of Uxbridge in 1938. Like the other surface stations on the Piccadilly Line northern extension the platforms were in a shallow cutting, but no attempt was made to create a majestic surface building as had been the case elsewhere. Instead a neat but modest single-storey entrance building led down to the sub-surface ticket hall with its glazed roof and to two island platforms. The middle track sat below a high glazed clerestory roof, shown above, while the roofs over the two outer tracks were just above car height.

By 1929 the Underground Group, spearheaded by Lord Ashfield, was promoting a co-ordination bill in Parliament aimed at creating a unified public transport system for London. A surprise change of government in 1929 stopped the bill in its tracks, along with a similar one being promoted by the London County Council, which controlled much of the Capital's tramways. A further change of government from Labour to National Coalition in 1931 brought in the Liberal Percy Pybus as Minister of Transport. He supported the London Passenger Transport Bill drawn up by Herbert Morrison under the previous Labour administration. Under this proposal a governing Board, under public control but strictly non-political, would plan and operate all bus, tram and Underground railway services within a designated area. The Board would not be subsidised, so services would be self-supporting. After a sometimes difficult passage through Parliament the Bill received Royal Assent on 13th April 1933. The legislation, important though it was, meant little change for the Underground railways, except for the Metropolitan, which lost its independent status and, with some considerable reluctance became, from Saturday 1st July 1933, part of the new London Passenger Transport Board's Underground railway system.

From now, our story is of a fully unified system. The momentum of growth and service improvements, which had characterised the London Underground in the years before the formation of the LPTB, continued into the new era and the Board was quick to stamp its authority on the proceedings. The legend LONDON TRANSPORT gradually replaced UNDERGROUND on Underground Group trains, and was soon applied to former Metropolitan stock as well, but a short-lived LPTB logo was quickly superseded by a modified version of the bar and circle symbol that had become so well known since its first use about 25 years earlier.

Underground improvements during the rest of 1933 and into 1934 were mostly the fruits of schemes started by the Underground Group, whose top management the new Board inherited. However, the very first new station to be served by Underground trains under London Transport ownership was the LMS-owned South Kenton, shared by Bakerloo Line trains, which opened on 3rd July. On the last day of the same month, the Piccadilly Line north London extension reached Cockfosters. On 18th September the remodelled Dover Street station opened. This consisted of a new sub-surface ticket hall, accessible by subway from both sides of Piccadilly and linked by new escalators to the existing platforms, which were now approached from their western end. The old Dover Street station entrance was closed and the station renamed, more appropriately, Green Park, as the 53 acre park lay to the south of one of the new station entrances. A few days later, on the 24th, British Museum station closed, being replaced from the following morning by new platforms for the Central London Railway at Holborn affording a direct subway and escalator link with the Piccadilly Line.

The last piece of the Piccadilly Line extension jigsaw fell into place on 23rd October when the line ran on from South Harrow over District tracks to Rayners Lane and then on to Uxbridge, replacing the District Line shuttle service over this section and bringing to an end District operation in north-west London.

Within a few months of taking over from the Underground Group, the LPTB asked general manager J. P. Thomas to look at the possibility of withdrawing first class accommodation on the Metropolitan, District and Great Northern & City Lines. He reported in December 1933 that it was too soon to end it on the Metropolitan and District but that first class could be abolished on the GN&C, the economies outweighing any loss of traffic that might result. The fears of Metropolitan staff and passengers that standards would fall under London Transport ownership were well founded, though it was not until the Second World War provided an excuse that the LPTB felt it could withdraw first class on this and the District.

On 21st January 1934 the shuttle service from Watford to Rickmansworth was withdrawn, and the two double-ended motor coaches used on the service were transferred to the Wembley Park–Stanmore branch where they ran an off-peak shuttle service. They continued to work in this form on the branch until February 1938.

New ticket hall at Knightsbridge station in March 1934, one month after being completed. The same programme of work included a new entrance opposite Harrods. This opened on 30th July 1934, enabling the closure of Brompton Road station, 500 yards to the west. A similar large ticket hall at Leicester Square was brought into use the following year. Brompton Road was the last Piccadilly Line station to be closed as a consequence of the 1930s extensions. The closure of Down Street in May 1932 and York Road in September of the same year had enabled faster journey times to be possible in the central area of the much extended Piccadilly Line.

The District Line service to Barking and beyond had been well patronised, especially since the opening of the extension to Upminster. Two additional stations had been built and opened by the LMS for District trains since 1932. Upminster Bridge had opened on 17th December 1934 with Elm Park following on 13th May 1935. There was an urgent need to increase peak hour capacity, at least as far as Barking. Some Hammersmith & City trains had been running as far as East Ham since 30th March 1936, but from 4th May the part of the Hammersmith & City which ran down to New Cross and New Cross Gate daily was diverted to Barking, giving the beleaguered stretch an additional eight trains an hour. The off-peak Hammersmith to New Cross or New Cross Gate service was diverted to terminate at Whitechapel. First class accommodation was abolished on both the Hammersmith & City and the East London Line from the same date, foreshadowing its general elimination on the Underground within a few years. Its continuation on the District Line had been the subject of protests (see right).

As mentioned earlier, tube trains began to be fitted with air operated sliding doors from 1923 after trials on the Piccadilly in 1921/22. On the Metropolitan, slam door stock was used, the last variation of this design being delivered in 1932. The District had employed hand operated sliding doors and up to 1936 these were universal on the District Line, the Hammersmith & City Line, the Circle Line and the East London Line. For the first new surface stock trains to be ordered by the London Passenger Transport Board, in 1935, air operated doors were specified for two of them on an experimental basis which were under the control of the guard at the rear of the train. Moving responsibility for closing the doors to the guard was seen as a way of enabling trains with higher acceleration to be introduced safely. On trains with handworked sliding doors it was not unknown for doors to be left open and for passengers to jump on a train moving out of the platform. There was also the temptation to leave a door or two open while the train was proceeding on its journey in very hot weather.

Nine new trains were delivered for service on the Hammersmith & City Line and District Line during the spring and summer of 1936 and were known as M and N classes, being built by the BRCW and Metro-Cammell respectively. Apart from the fitting of air-door equipment to part of the order, they were similar to the UCC-built L stock of 1932 and were the last trains on the Underground to be built with clerestory roofs. Most of the M class entered service on 4th May 1936 in time for the extra peak train service to Barking.

An M-stock motor car, built for the Hammersmith & City section of the Metropolitan Line, is seen here when new in May 1936. This car was one of the very last on the Underground to be fitted with hand-operated passenger doors. It displays a line identification transfer, a short-lived mid-1930s idea.

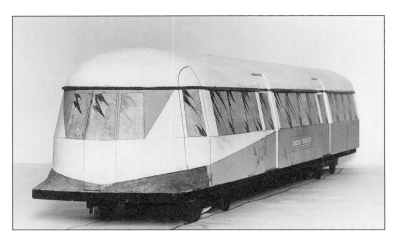

A significant event took place on 8th April 1937 with the entry into service on the Piccadilly Line of the first all new design of tube train for 15 years. Early in 1933, some experiments had been carried out using standard stock cars to test streamline aerodynamics, new air conditioning equipment, and automatic and mechanical couplers. These pioneering tests apart, the main feature of the new train and the greatest departure from former practice was the position of the electrical equipment which was placed entirely beneath the car floors instead of in a separate compartment inside the motor-cars, thereby freeing-up more space for passenger seating. The first train, comprising six motor-cars, was delivered from Metro-Cammell to London Transport at the end of 1936. It was followed during 1937 by 18 other cars built principally to the same specification but with different traction equipment. By having each car motored, acceleration surpassed anything that had gone before. Each car was 52ft 6ins long. There were two sets of air-operated double doors and a single-leaf door on each side. Roofs were elliptical. The windows were flush fitting and there was a total absence of panel beading below roof level. The first two cars were air-conditioned and had double-glazed windows throughout, while the others had conventional opening windows fitted.

The handsome lines of the 1935 tube-stock brought to the tube the concept of streamlining, which was then in vogue on anything from express steam locomotives to saloon cars. The new trains followed closely the designer's original thoughts, manifested in a 1934 mock-up (above).

But the most dramatic feature of the first 18 cars was the streamlined cab ends. In the mid-1930s streamlining was very much in vogue and all the Big Four railway companies had dabbled with streamlined steam locomotives to varying degrees. The cabs on the 1935 tube stock, as it came to be called, were bay-fronted with the side cab doors set at an angle within the bay. The bay contained a front cab door and two side windows, separated from the side doors by thick pillars inset with a panel containing the train running number. In the front cab door were five square code lights and the train destination screen. The cab was topped with a domed roof containing a 'v' shaped air-inlet ventilator.

The driver's position in the cab was central, with 'joystick' controls replacing the conventional handles. One of the six-car trains differed in as much as it had a more conventional cab design and layout. Gone was any attempt at streamlining. The cab was flat-ended and shallower than the streamlined cabs, allowing for two additional seats in the passenger saloon. The code lights and destination screen were in the conventional position under the offside front window. All 24 had been delivered by the end of October 1937 and the last train, made up of the three flat-fronted sets, entered service on the Piccadilly Line early in 1938 by which time a huge fleet of new tube trains, sufficient to tackle the additional service authorised under the New Works Programme, was on order.

The streamlined 1935 stock at work, the presence of more than one person in the cab suggesting a first day photo.

Sloane Square station was modernised at the beginning of the war with the provision of escalators, unique in connecting a Circle Line platform by this means to street level. This end of the station, including the street level building, was destroyed by a bomb on 12th November 1940, giving this work a very short life indeed.

An overnight heavy bombing attack on the City of London on 29th/30th December, called by some the Second Fire of London, included the destruction of Moorgate station and a train parked overnight in one of the platforms.

The tube shelterers were sometimes visited by popular entertainers; in this case comedy singer and ukulele player George Formby.

At the end of 1940, after only two stages had been completed and opened, building work on the various Northern Line extensions was suspended. All references to them were removed from the Underground map at the same time. On 19th January 1941 the new Highgate station opened. It was not finished, and at its opening passengers had to walk up a flight of stairs from the ticket hall to the street, a climb regulars would have to endure until one of the planned escalators was installed in 1957. The platforms at Highgate, the design and decoration of which followed those at St John's Wood and Swiss Cottage on the Bakerloo, could accommodate nine-car trains, but these had ceased operating at the start of the war and were destined never to resume.

The streamlined 1935 stock was mothballed during the war, though not before a revised front end design had been tried out on one of the units. The streamlined design was not popular, with drivers and the modified version was even less popular. The trains never ran in service again.

A cut-away artist's impression of how the completed Highgate station might have looked, although the artist, D. Macpherson, has chosen to keep the surface platforms in the hands of LNER trains rather than the planned Northern Line services to Alexandra Palace. A sculpture of Dick Whittington and his cat was planned for the main Archway Road entrance, but the legend's return to Highgate was never to be realised. As plans stood, Highgate was to be a key interchange on the fully fledged Northern Line, serving trains which had come from the Bank and Charing Cross branches at deep level, and trains which had come from the extended Northern City Line north of Finsbury Park en route to Alexandra Palace at surface level. A new station interchange complex had been designed and almost completed when the work was stopped.

By the end of 1951 work was under way on the second phase of the R stock programme for the District Line. Post-war shortages of steel had caused LT to consider the use of aluminium as an alternative material for carriage panelling. During the war LT engineers had worked with aluminium in aircraft construction, and it seemed appropriate to consider its use again in the light of the steel shortage. An order for 90 new aluminium bodied cars of R stock (six motor-cars and 84 NDMs) was placed with Metro-Cammell in 1949 with Gloucester undertaking the work of converting 49 more Q38 trailers to motor-cars.

The new carriages were classified R49 and very similar in appearance to the previous deliveries of R stock. LT was anxious to see if any cost savings emerged by operating the lighter aluminium cars. Although the building contract specified that the new stock be painted in the traditional red, it occurred to the engineers that even more weight would be saved by not painting the car exteriors; aluminium alloy being anti-corrosive did not require traditional painting. In August 1951 two motor-cars, one 1938 tube stock and a P stock, were each fitted with aluminium alloy body panels, part polished, part sanded. After undergoing trials for several weeks without any apparent adverse effects it was decided to ask Metro-Cammell to leave one completed R49 car unpainted. The car was delivered in April 1952 and entered service two months later. Public reaction was favourable and LT asked Metro-Cammell to deliver sufficient unpainted cars to enable a complete 'silver' train, including two unpainted R49 motor-cars, to be made up. The only relief to the expanse of silver-coloured alloy was a red band beneath the window line which continued around the front of the train cabs.

As the new trains were entering service on the District a major rehabilitation of the F stock was nearing completion. The work began soon after the F stock was transferred to the Metropolitan with the first cars being dealt with in September 1951. Aluminium alloy doors replaced the original wood and steel doors. The cars were rewired, repanelled where necessary, better lighting and new seating were installed, and passenger door control was fitted. The programme was completed in December 1953 and contributed to the F stock being fit for a further ten years.

In June 1955, following problems with the Metadyne control system used on the P stock trains working on the Circle Line, London Transport decided to replace it with the more reliable Pneumatic Camshaft Mechanism (PCM) control equipment used in the 1938 tube stock. The first train so fitted was ready for service in April 1956, and initial results showed an improvement in train reliability. Gradually the rest of the O/P fleet lost its Metadyne control in favour of PCM equipment, a process that took until 1965 to complete.

The prototype unpainted aluminium car in a District Line train in 1952. Complete trains of unpainted aluminium finish followed.

Silver Trains Galore

The oldest standard stock was by now approaching its thirty-fifth birthday and was thus becoming due for replacement. A new design was on the drawing board. 'New' may be a generous description because the design was, to the layman, aluminium bodied 1938 stock without the domed cab roof. The prototype trains comprised seven cars (M–T–NDM–M+M–T–M). The most outstanding feature of all three, and the one which caught the headlines, was their unpainted 'silver' finish, LT having now decided to build all future rolling-stock of aluminium alloy panelling which was to be left unpainted. Other developments from the 1938 stock design were that a destination indicator box was positioned above the front cab door and roof mounted door operation indicator lights alerted the guard to any doors which had not closed properly at stations. Internally things were a little different from the 1938 styling. Transverse seating in the centre bays faced the corresponding opposite seat. The red and grey moquette was in a pattern of straight lines and used alongside blue-grey paintwork. Ceilings were white and along the length of each ran dual strip lighting, which made the car interiors extremely bright. The interior colour scheme and the use of fluorescent lighting transformed the insides from the homely feel of 1938 tube stock to a colder, office-like environment.

A batch of 76 seven-car aluminium bodied tube trains of similar design to the prototypes was ordered from Metro-Cammell and entered service on the Piccadilly Line on 14th December 1959. This was the start of the 1959 tube stock programme. Under it, all the Piccadilly Line's standard stock would be replaced, and some of the newer 1927–1934 cars transferred to the Central to replace the 1923–26 vintage standard stock until it received new trains. Spare cars would be used to make up the remaining seven-car trains on the Central to eight cars. The raw unpainted livery remained, relieved only by a dove grey roof, changed to gloss black early on in the production run.

The need to provide some extra trains for the District Line, as well as increasing the length of Circle Line trains from five to six cars, set the planners' minds working in the late 1950s. The option eventually decided upon involved converting seventeen Q38 trailers to O/P trailers to increase the length of Circle Line trains to six cars, and converting a further seven Q38 trailers into R38 motor-cars to run with 13 new aluminium bodied NDMs (R59 stock) ordered from Metro-Cammell to the 1949 pattern. They were delivered between July and September 1959. All were left unpainted, and the newly converted R38 motor cars were painted silver to match. During 1956/57 five other R stock cars had been painted silver to match the original unpainted car No.23567, creating two 'silver' trains on the District. Following the arrival of the R59 cars, and the conversion of the Q38 trailers to motors, there were, technically, three more. All the R59 stock was in service by the end of October 1959.

Electrification of British Railways services into Liverpool Street in the late 1950s brought with it the prospect of more traffic on the Central Line. The updating of the Central Line's train fleet therefore acquired some urgency. The original plan had been to renew the Piccadilly fleet with new 1959 stock trains and transfer the best of its standard stock to the Central to replace cars of 1923–26 vintage until brand new trains for the Central were delivered. The arrival of prototypes of the new trains planned for the line was still some months off, so full production would be a couple of years away. A quick solution to meet the increased demand was the allocation to the Central of the last 57 trains of 1959 stock then being delivered for the Piccadilly. An extra 57 non-driving motor cars were ordered to make the seven-car trains up to the eight cars needed for the Central. To give the Central Line its own fleet of modern rolling stock, an order for 84½ new trains similar to the 1959 stock was placed with the Birmingham Railway Carriage & Wagon Company and the BR works at Derby. These (the 1962 stock) would run on the Central Line enabling 1959 stock to return to the Piccadilly.

Leading in this photograph is a 1938 built car painted silver to match as closely as possible the unpainted aluminium trailers of later build coupled to it.

One of the first 12 prototype driving motor cars hauling its rehabilitated Standard Stock trailers. The external design of the double width windows would be perpetuated for the next 23 years on coachbuilt tube stock. The slightly raked back stance of the cab windows was effectively resolved by carrying through the body side crease line through to the front. The reconditioned Standard Stock trailer cars which were used to make up complete trains can be seen. They were painted to match the unpainted motor cars as closely as possible.

Some elements of the pre-war New Works Programme took time to reach fruition. Work on the four-tracking of the Metropolitan Line from Harrow to Rickmansworth, and the onward electrification to Amersham and Chesham, suspended during the war, did not resume until 1959. The immense task of lengthening and widening 17 bridges and laying new tracks, all within a distance of six and a half miles, continued during 1960. The electrification to Amersham and Chesham was completed first, and on 15th August 1960 the first electric train, composed of T stock, ran under test to Amersham. A new fleet of 31 unpainted aluminium eight-car trains (A60 stock) had been ordered from Cravens of Sheffield for the replacement of all trains on the Amersham, Chesham and Watford branches of the Met.

On Monday 12th September 1960 the steam era on the Metropolitan began slipping away with the operation of the last steam-hauled train on the Chesham branch. The quaint Ashbury coaches used on the push-pull service for over 60 years were withdrawn, four of them, happily in the new age of railway preservation, finding a new home on the Bluebell Railway in Sussex. The steam service to Aylesbury, operated by British Railways (London Midland Region) on London Transport's behalf, continued two more years. Looking ahead to future train services on the Metropolitan, LT ordered a further 216 cars from Cravens, making up 27 eight-car trains, to replace the F and P stocks on the Uxbridge branch.

The first of the twelve prototype motor-cars that had originally been intended to test concepts for the new Central Line fleet arrived from Cravens in June 1960. After evaluation and testing the first train went into service on Wednesday 9th November. London Transport now intended to use the cars as a test bed for the next generation of tube train. The 1960 tube stock embodied many new features. Each bogie was equipped with two traction motors connected in permanent series. The motor-cars could couple to any other motor-car of the same type regardless of whether it was A or D end in either direction, a useful feature on the Central Line with the Hainault loop necessitating standard coupling units being kept facing the same direction. The new cars had three bays on each side each containing two large 'double' windows instead of the usual four. These windows were double glazed. The aluminium body panels tapered inwards from waist level on both sides of the cars, and at the front end. The cab had a domed roof containing a destination indicator box. The three eight-car trains created by the twelve new motor-cars offered an interesting contrast in styles. Instead of building twelve new trailers to run with them, twelve standard stock trailers (four built by MCW in 1927, and eight by BRCW and GRCW dating from 1931), were refurbished, including the installation of fluorescent lighting. All were painted silver to closely match the new motor-cars in unpainted aluminium.

HRH Princess Alexandra officially opened the Brixton extension of the Victoria Line on Friday 23rd July 1971. The Princess unveiled a plaque at Brixton before making a return trip to see the progress being made on Pimlico station, which had started after work on the main extension had begun. The stations on the extension were in the same style as those on the original Victoria Line. Passing through the still being built station at Pimlico, the first stop on the new extension was Vauxhall, where there was an interchange with the BR (Southern) station. The platforms, which were in the same style as others on the Victoria Line, had a motif depicting an ornamental trellis from the Vauxhall Gardens, which had closed in 1859. At the next station, Stockwell, there was interchange with the Northern Line. Here it was even possible to provide cross-platform interchange because the Northern Line platforms at Stockwell had been built outside the running tunnels. The wall motif consisted of blue zigzag lines. The original ticket hall was enlarged and a new escalator installed in readiness for the Victoria Line.

Brixton, the southern terminus, was a modest affair, especially considering that it would have a vital role as a huge railhead for people reaching the tube from a wide area. The ticket hall was reached by steps from the entrance in Brixton Road. Two escalators took passengers to and from the now familiar style platform. Perhaps inspiration had deserted the designers of the station motif. In tile on the platform walls was simply a ton of bricks, a visual pun on the name Brixton. A new tunnel extension further south provided overnight stabling for two trains. During 1970 five new covered sidings had been added to Northumberland Park depot in readiness for the additional trains ordered for the extension to Brixton.

By the end of 1971, 969 new tube cars were either being built or on order. In addition to the 210 for the Northern Line, (1972 Mark I stock), a further order for 231 cars of the same type (1972 Mark II stock) had been placed, ultimately for the Fleet Line but initially to work on the Northern. The remaining 528 cars would form 88 six-car trains for the Piccadilly Line to commence delivery in 1973, orders for which were placed with Metro-Cammell in 1971. Their arrival would enable the 1959 stock to transfer to the Northern Line to replace the last of the line's 1938 tube stock. A backlog of maintenance of this now elderly stock had occurred during a lengthy strike at Acton Works between September and December 1969, leading to the Northern Line being dubbed 'The Misery Line' when a third of its trains were out of action.

In April 1970, the first unit of the Hammersmith & City and Circle Line replacement stock, coded C69 (C for Circle) arrived from Metro-Cammell. The car bodies were to a new design, having four sets of double-doors on each side to facilitate quicker boarding and alighting. The cars seated 32. One interesting feature of the new trains was the provision for future conversion to automatic control. The first entered service on 28th September 1970 allowing the gradual displacement of CO/CP trains to the District where a start was then made on withdrawing the Q stock, dating back to the 1920s.

In the midst of these new developments the last clerestory roofed train on the Underground ran in passenger service on the District Line on the evening of Friday 24th September 1971. A special farewell tour took place for enthusiasts on the 26th.

Triumphs and Tragedies

On 14th September 1972 the final piece in the Victoria Line jigsaw fell into place when the new Pimlico station opened. The tiled station entrance led to a sub-surface ticket hall and thence by escalators to the platforms. The tile motif, set into the wall behind the platform seats consisted of yellow dots on a white background, a reflection of the modern art in the nearby Tate Gallery.

In February 1972 work began on building the Fleet Line, the first excavations being in the Trafalgar Square and Strand area. The intention was to use these tunnels as sidings until a decision was reached on the future extension of the line. During the spring contracts were placed for 2¾ miles of tunnel between Baker Street and Strand. In April work began on a reconstruction of Bond Street station with an enlarged ticket hall, a new concourse and the excavation of two new escalator shafts. A 600 tonne steel umbrella was erected at the junction of Oxford Street and Davies Street to enable work on the new ticket hall to be carried out beneath without disrupting road traffic. A scheme to reconstruct Strand station with a large new ticket hall and the provision of three escalators to replace the lifts was approved by the GLC. Eventually it was to link up with Trafalgar Square to create a whole new station complex to be called Charing Cross. During the 1973 Easter Holiday an umbrella bridge was erected across the forecourt of Charing Cross (BR) station to allow for the building of the large ticket hall planned for the new Charing Cross station complex. A further development was the complete closure of Strand station from 17th June 1973 in preparation for the opening of the new Charing Cross station complex, when the intention was to rename the existing Charing Cross station Embankment.

In February 1973 the Ministry of Transport and the GLC set up a London Rail Study to look at the problems facing London's railways before the turn of the century and to make recommendations. The Study published a report the following year, which forecast that over £2 billion would need to be spent during the period on the existing rail network and new services, if London's railways were to play their part in meeting the future needs of the Capital. As far as the Underground was concerned, the report recommended the extension of the Fleet Line from Strand via Fenchurch Street and Docklands, then earmarked for redevelopment, and on to Woolwich and Thamesmead, where a huge new residential development was being built. It also suggested a line from Chelsea to Hackney which, by adding the Wimbledon branch of the District and the Leytonstone to Hainault branch of the Central Line, would create a new south-west to north-east tube line. This idea had been first mooted by LT in January 1970. Among the other proposals was a deep level 'CrossRail' link from east to west to create a line from Shenfield in Essex to Aylesbury/Reading. This would be operated by British Rail. Forty years later CrossRail was in course of construction.

The first of the 1973 tube stock trains for the Piccadilly Line arrived at West Ruislip from Metro-Cammell on 16th August 1974. The cars were longer than older tube stocks, being 57ft 4ins (motor cars) and 58ft (trailers), against 52ft 9ins and 52ft 5ins for the motor cars and trailers of the 1972 stocks. This reduced building costs because each train could be formed of six cars. It was a policy that was to be followed from now on. Externally they resembled the 1967/1972 stocks apart from a slightly different cab profile. The lower section of the cab was painted red, the only relief from the predominant external silver. The stock was built for eventual one-person operation (OPO), but initially a guard's control panel was provided in the driver's cab. Internally the colour scheme was as the 1972 MkII stock, except for the cab end wall and saloon cab door which was bright yellow. The door screens were repositioned to allow cases to be stood by the doors.

Once a passenger had actually entered a London tube train, he or she would expect to be treading on traditional maple wood flooring. But by 1974 maple was becoming expensive and difficult to obtain so LT experimented with some alternatives, including vinyl tiling and even carpet! A 1959 stock car (No.9153) was chosen for the latter experiment, bringing carpet back to the Underground for the first time since the withdrawal of the first class compartments on the Metropolitan back in 1940. The 1974 experiment was not regarded as a success, and the traditional wood flooring was to remain a feature of the London Underground train for the next twenty years.

In 1975 the Underground catered for 601 million passenger journeys. Although this was a reduction of 36 million over the total for 1974, it was still a creditable number, and the fact that in its 112-year history there had been so few mishaps only served to illustrate how generally safe the system was. Fatalities connected with train accidents were, and are, very rare on the Underground. In fact in the 42 years since the formation of London Transport there had been only two accidents involving passenger fatalities. At the end of the morning rush hour on 17th May 1938 there was a collision between Charing Cross and Temple stations when a Circle Line train ran into the back of a District train held at a stop signal. Six people died and damage to the wooden carriages was considerable. The cause was a wrongly wired signal circuit, which had given the Circle train a green light to proceed. Fifteen years later, just before 7pm on 8th April 1953, an Epping bound Central Line train ran into the back of the preceding train which was stationary in the tunnel between Stratford and Leyton. Trains in the area were being delayed because of a signal failure. Twelve passengers were killed and many others injured, including the driver of the Epping train, who was held largely to blame by the subsequent Public Inquiry for not carrying out strict observance of the 'stop and proceed' rule which had to be applied during signal failures.

At the end of 1972 work was well advanced on the Piccadilly Line extension to Heathrow. At Hounslow West, a new below-ground island platform was being built by the cut-and-cover method to replace the surface terminus platforms. Island platforms were also provided at Hatton Cross and Heathrow Central and the construction site for the latter had a fairly accurate representation of 1973 tube stock on its hoardings.

A new design consultant appointed by London Transport in 1970 specified a single colour roundel for all applications – including Underground station signs. All-red roundels were trialled at Sloane Square towards the end of 1971 but they were not well received and the traditional blue bar was reinstated after a short time.

The first phase of the development of a new automated ticketing system came into being on 31st October 1982 when prototype equipment, consisting of ticket machines and gates, was introduced at Vauxhall station. The system's main aim was to reduce ticket fraud. It included two types of passenger-operated ticket machine; one called a Tenfare, selling the ten most popular single tickets, and an Allfare, which issued credit card sized single, return and cheap-day return tickets to all Underground stations. Both machines gave change. They were wall-mounted, and staff could service them from within the ticket office, thus removing the need to come out into the ticket hall to empty the machines of cash. The ticket gates were reversible, and could check season tickets as well. It was intended that evaluation of the new system would enable LT to decide on the adoption of a suitable system for the whole Underground. The Vauxhall experiment ran until July 1983, and the experience gained had proved valuable, enabling LT to decide how to take the project forward. A £100 million package was drawn up which included ticket gates for Zone 1 stations, the installation system-wide of automated wall-mounted ticket issuing machines selling a range of tickets, secure ticket offices for staff, and a Penalty Fare system with increased ticket checking on trains. The next stage of the project was to evaluate different ticket issuing equipment. In May 1985 the Transport Secretary approved a £135 million expenditure programme for the new ticketing system in line with the plans set out after the successful Vauxhall trials. On 22nd May 1983 ticket zones were introduced across the whole Underground within Greater London, to simplify ticket issue. There were five zones 1, 2, 3A, 3B and 3C, the three 'Zone 3s' being regarded as one zone for bus travel, and tickets were priced depending on the number of zones passed through on each journey. The Travelcard, which included availability on LT bus services was introduced with this fare revision, and was an immediate success, far out-stripping the previous point-to-point season ticket sales. In fact the Travelcard became so popular that between April 1986 and April 1987 the Underground catered for 769 million passenger journeys. This was in stark contrast to the doldrum period post-Fares Fare in 1982 when the total was 482 million.

In September 1981, the GLC had announced approval of a £60 million ten-year rolling programme to modernise 140 stations, sixteen of them receiving major face-lifts accounting for two-thirds of the overall cost. By the end of that year work had begun on the first four projects, the Bakerloo ticket hall at Charing Cross, and the Central Line escalators and platforms at Tottenham Court Road, Oxford Circus and Bond Street. The modernised Bakerloo ticket hall at Charing Cross reopened on 13th December 1983. The platforms were unveiled at the same time. They had been modernised with murals comprising sections of paintings from the nearby National and National Portrait Galleries. One of the most striking was a scene from Henri Rousseau's 'Tropical Storm With Tiger'.

R stock last ran in passenger service in March 1983, but the flare-sided stock continued in use on the Underground for a time in the shape of Q38 pilot motor cars L126 and L127, seen at Acton Works in July 1983 in the company of engineers' vehicles converted from standard stock and 1903 Central London Railway stock. The last D stock entered service on the District Line on 15th July 1983. The District main line services were now operated with a fleet of trains all of the same design for the first time in 70 years.

The first unit of the order for fifteen 1983 tube stock six-car trains for the Jubilee Line arrived at Neasden depot from Metro-Cammell on 27th August. As on the D stock the passenger sliding doors were single leaf; a design feature subsequently felt to have been a mistake. One new feature inside was the concealed lighting. The fluorescent tubes were fixed behind frosted covers, which apart from providing the main in-car illumination also illuminated the advertising posters. There was also public address and train radio to enable the driver to speak to the line controller, both features then becoming the norm throughout the Underground fleet. The first train of 1983 tube stock entered service on Tuesday 1st May 1984 to convey special guests to a celebration of the Jubilee Line's fifth birthday.

The controversial change to one-person-operation (OPO) of trains on the Underground moved a step closer in early 1984 when the Trade Unions agreed to a twelve week trial on the Hammersmith & City Line. The experiment, which began on 26th March, was slow to settle down, with much late running. Passengers waiting for long periods on the Hammersmith & City platforms at Baker Street could at least marvel at the latest station modernisation project, unveiled on 10th April. 'Modernisation' is perhaps not the right word; 're-creation' would be better, because the platforms had been restored to their 1863 glory. All the old wall panelling had been removed to reveal the original brickwork which was carefully restored. When the station was built, natural light shone through shafts in the roof, and to recreate the daylight effect the shafts were lined inside with white tile and illuminated from above. The base of the shafts provided a fine location for platform seating and the station name frieze. The conversion of the Circle Line to OPO was implemented on 22nd October 1984 with the District following on 4th November 1985.

1983 stock with 1972 stock far right in the Stanmore sidings of the Jubilee Line.

1986 was the Government's target year for the dissolution of the Greater London Council. A right-wing Conservative government and a left-wing Labour-run GLC could hardly be a marriage made in Heaven, and since the Fares Fare debacle relations between the Palace of Westminster and County Hall had been far from harmonious. The Government planned to hand over most of the functions necessary to run London to the individual borough councils, but transport was a different matter, and the Government was anxious to wrest control of London Transport from the GLC before the 1986 dissolution. The Government believed that private enterprise should be given an opportunity to participate in providing services to public transport, particularly on the buses. To this end it introduced new legislation in the form of the London Regional Transport Act, which received Royal Assent on 26th June 1984. The LRT Act created a Corporation, London Regional Transport, which in turn was charged with setting-up wholly owned subsidiaries to run the various elements of London's public transport, including the Underground. Little time was wasted in bringing in the new order, for at midnight on 29th June 1984 London Regional Transport replaced the London Transport Executive in name only, but with a new reporting line to the Transport Minister. There then followed a period of several months when LRT was directly responsible for the operation of the Underground and the buses, while the new subsidiaries were being set up. On Monday 1st April 1985, LRT's new subsidiaries came into being. Out of all the new subsidiaries London Underground Limited (LUL) was probably the least affected by the change. The new bus subsidiary, London Buses Limited, soon found itself in the forefront of competition under the new rules for bus route tendering. LUL had its own management structure under Chairman and Managing Director, Dr Tony Ridley. LRT became an overall planning body which, among other things set fare levels.

The platforms at Holborn were modernised with large panels depicting exhibits in the nearby British Museum.

The process of modernising and redecorating the principal stations on the network continued with work at Leicester Square, Holborn, Piccadilly Circus, Paddington and Finsbury Park beginning during 1984. Work was also under way on the Oxford Circus Bakerloo Line platforms where, in common with the situation at other sites, the contractor's materials were stored in a hoarded-off cross-passageway. On the evening of 23rd November a fire broke out in this area, gutting the northbound Victoria Line platform, and its associated cross-passageways with the Bakerloo Line. Many passengers were taken to hospital with smoke inhalation. The Victoria Line was suspended between Warren Street and Victoria until 17th December. The cause was thought to have been a discarded cigarette end or match, and a ban on smoking which had been introduced on trains on 9th July 1984 was extended, from 17th February 1985, to cover platforms, subways and booking halls of stations which were all or partly below ground.

At Baker Street, the aim was to re-create the atmosphere of the original platforms from 1863. The original ventilation shafts, long since covered over, were fitted with lighting to give a sense of the daylight that would originally have shone down these.

white side panelling with a blue skirt, and grey roofs. Under the first phase of the project the C stock and the 1967/1972 (MkII) stocks were to be refurbished. No Government money was yet available to make the same transformation to the 1973 tube stock or the A stock, although trial refurbishments were on display to show what could be achieved. All the trains had improved communications in the form of better public address.

The C stock was refurbished by RFS at Doncaster under a contract awarded in 1990, while the 1967/72 tube stock was refurbished by Tickford Rail at the Royal Rosyth Dockyard. In April 1992 a contract for the refurbishment of the A stock was awarded to BREL in Derby. The first refurbished A stock trains entered service on the Metropolitan Line in September 1994. These trains, the oldest of which were already nearly 35 years old, were to last almost 20 years longer.

On 1st July 1991 the Docklands Light Railway was extended to Bank. The huge complex at Bank/Monument was the City's busiest station and here one of the biggest station modernisation projects was under way. It had begun in 1991 and was of such magnitude that it took seven years to complete. Every square inch of the station complex, three ticket halls, six platforms, 15 escalators, four lifts, and a labyrinth of subways, was to be refurbished. The DLR was linked to all parts of the complex, adding more subways and escalators to those already there.

The impressive line-up of refurbished trains await inspection by those who can sanction the expenditure for a large-scale refurbishment programme. The scene at Rickmansworth sidings on 16th July 1991.

Interior of the refurbished C stock, giving a much more spacious feel compared to the design when new – albeit at the expense of the transverse seating.

On 17th September 1992 Angel station reopened after a £70 million rebuilding scheme. A large new entrance and ticket hall had been built in Islington High Street to replace the original one in City Road. The old station with its worn-out lifts gave way to a bright, modern and spacious station, everything an efficient tube station should be. From the ticket hall three escalators, the longest on the Underground with a vertical rise of 27.425 metres, led down to an intermediate level. From there three shorter (8.32 metre) escalators led down to the platforms. The southbound platform is the original island platform with the northbound track filled in to create a wider waiting area. A completely new northbound platform was built, clad in vitreous enamel and marble, the marble extending to subways and the ticket hall. On 23rd October 1992 Mornington Crescent station closed for refurbishment and the replacement of its original 1907 lifts. It was to remain closed for almost six years.

On 26th November 1991 LU launched a radical and far-reaching Company Plan. The Monopolies and Mergers Commission had acknowledged in a June 1991 report that the Underground had suffered from chronic under-investment over many years, making it impossible for the Company to keep essential infrastructure up to date. More funding was promised from central Government, both in the immediate and long term. London Underground was expected to play its part by running an efficient and more cost-effective operation, and more than £700 million in cost savings were identified. To implement these savings some major changes to staffing levels and organisation were proposed. For the first time some of the Underground support services, like cleaning and train maintenance, were to be offered out to the private sector under tender. A large-scale reorganisation of station and train management structures resulted in a staff reduction of around 5,000 during the following four years. The plan touched all areas of LU's operation, including safety, train services, maintenance and signalling; but the emphasis was on customer focused accountability and performance measures, which were regularly published through a Customer Charter launched in August 1992.

The first of the 85 trains of 1992 tube stock entered passenger service on the Central Line on 7th April 1993, running initially only during off-peaks between West Ruislip and Liverpool Street. Peak hour appearances had to wait until June. Deliveries had begun on 17th May 1992. The build of the stock was based on the 1986 prototype. The bodies are constructed of welded aluminium panels, thus saving weight and cost. Passenger and driver side cab doors are pneumatically operated and externally hung, to save giving the car bodies a double-skin. Each motor car has two sets of double-doors and one single-leaf door, while the trailer cars have a single-leaf door at each end. The double-doors open to give 1.66 metres entry space, the widest so far on a London Underground train. The cars have end windows to increase vision and security. These had been introduced on refurbished cars of the Victoria Line 1967 stock, but the 1992 stock was the first new fleet of trains to have them and the feature is now standard on new Underground rolling stock. Also now standard are the warning beeps which sound just before the doors close – though previously most passengers had the intelligence to detect this was going to happen when they heard the click of the pneumatic door motors. The Central Line had been involved in an experiment 45 years earlier in which sirens, hand-operated by platform staff, were sounded at Liverpool Street station 25 seconds after a train had arrived to hurry any passengers still about to board. It did not extend to any other stations.

Work on the Central Line modernisation, which was to be plagued with serious technical problems, was well under way by the start of 1993. New coded track circuit based signalling was being installed and commissioned at various locations. It had serious teething troubles which contributed to many years of service issues while the line's modernisation was sorted out.

For most of the twentieth century, technology changed only slowly. Traction supply, signalling and train control systems were still using technology in the 1980s that would have been recognisable to those who originally built the electric lines. When new technology eventually beckoned in the early 1980s it presented options for improving the Central Line and in 1985 a planning team was set up. The signalling dated back to the 1930s and was life expired, becoming unreliable and was constraining the ability to run more frequent services at a time where demand was increasing. However, service improvements could not be delivered with the existing trains, which at that time were less than 25 years old and probably had another ten years life in them. It was recognized that if the stock were replaced earlier this would coincide with the new signalling, opening up the possibility of automatic train operation and delivering benefits much sooner. The goal was 33 trains an hour through Liverpool Street in the morning peak (from 30) though if the upgrade were not pursued it was thought throughput would fall because of congestion. This kind of step-change improvement also meant upgrading electrical equipment (facilitating the use of regenerative braking for the first time since the 1930s) control and communication systems and some track (with alterations to track layout and reduced speed restrictions).

Large windows at the ends of each car of 1992 tube stock gave added security for passengers. All new tube trains have these as standard and some refurbished older stock has also been equipped.

This approach became known as 'line upgrade'. It was in theory the best way of delivering a fit-for-purpose railway. There were two problems. First, it hadn't been done before and required an unusually large project delivery process: upgrading an existing railway in daily service is even more difficult than building an entirely new one. Secondly, there was the complication of funding such an upgrade. For both these reasons it was a painful time. The first stage was obtaining prototype trains, delivered in 1986. Once planning was completed and costs and benefits understood, government authority to proceed was sought in summer 1988 (granted in October). It was initially costed at £550 million for completion in early 1996, but within two years it was re-costed at £750 million. Physical works began in 1990 but lingered until 2001, some signalling not complete until 2005. The overspend was enormous.

The financial problem was the Underground's volatile funding, settled annually and subject to violent change at short notice. Vast projects such as Central Line upgrade could not be accelerated or cut back to match funding yet took up such a large proportion of available capital in a poor year that it prejudiced funding of other essential work. The situation became so intolerable that a similar upgrade for the

Exterior view of the Central Line's 1992 stock just after delivery.

Northern Line was cut back to mere train provision, with existing signalling soldiering on for another two decades. Line upgrade did not return to the agenda until the Public Private Partnership arrived in 2003; intended to overcome this funding issue it introducing its own problems.

Trials with the new trains continued, one actually being sent to Ongar in July. But the locals at North Weald were mistaken if they thought their bit of the Central Line was in line for the new trains. In May new proposals were announced for the closure of the Epping-Ongar branch; they came a few months after a similar announcement of the intention to close the Aldwych branch. Objections were received to both proposals so they went to Public Inquiry. Permission for closure of both was granted by the Secretary of State for Transport on 1st September 1994 and both last operated on the final day or that month.

The last guard on the Underground on the last journey on 27th January 2000. Many are on board the train to celebrate the historic occasion. Note the advertising on the straphangers, a short-lived exercise in raising a bit more revenue.

One welcome measure from the Government had been a £1 billion investment package launched under the banner 'Tube 2000'. Every line was to benefit from the funding through projects covering many vital aspects of operations, including track and escalator upgrading, better communications, safety and station refurbishment. In July 1999, the Government awarded an additional £517 million to enable more vital improvements to be made on the Underground. LU quickly drew up a spending list, which was announced at a special meeting at London Transport's 55 Broadway Headquarters on 22nd July attended by Prime Minister Tony Blair and Deputy Prime Minister John Prescott. Improvements to train services on the Northern Line, track upgrades on the Bakerloo, Victoria and Metropolitan lines, infrastructure works, escalator refurbishment, step-free access for mobility impaired passengers at many stations, more CCTV and Help Points, and schemes to end overcrowding at Vauxhall, Brixton, Russell Square and Knightsbridge. The Government also endorsed LU's plans to reorganise its operations in preparation for PPP. The reorganisation was implemented on 18th September 1999 with the company being divided into the parts which would remain in public ownership (Opscos) being separated from those which would be controlled by the private sector (Infracos). The whole reorganisation was based around three line groupings, the Bakerloo, Central and Victoria lines, Jubilee, Northern and Piccadilly, and finally the sub-surface lines. The private sector consortiums would bid for ownership of one of the three Infracos based around the line groupings.

On 12th June 1999 work began on the first major piece of engineering work under the Tube 2000 investment banner. The tunnel roof on the section of the Circle Line between High Street Kensington and Gloucester Road needed strengthening, and the only way it could be achieved was to close the section of line for nine weeks. The Circle Line resumed on 23rd August, by which time a further large slice of engineering was under way on the Northern Line's Bank branch, which had been closed for tunnel strengthening in 1996. This time the target was the track, which was to be upgraded so that a number of permanent speed restrictions could be removed. Some tunnel enlargement work was also carried out. The section from Kennington to Moorgate was closed from 5th July until 6th September.

In May 1999 the Central Line's new communication system took a giant leap forward and the platform dot-matrix destination indicators, which had been misleading passengers with incorrect information for the past five years, were activated to show the correct destinations and arrival time of the next three trains. In September the new Wood Lane Control Centre began controlling the signalling on the western side of the line from Bank, and by the end of 1999 the Centre was controlling signalling as far east as Newbury Park. In December the training of Central Line train drivers for Automatic Train Operation began.

At Wembley Park it became necessary to make major changes to the station to update facilities and to cope adequately with the traffic to the new stadium. The work was undertaken by Tubelines on behalf of London Underground and received funding contributions from the stadium developer and the Mayor's single regeneration budget. This particular modernisation has proved to be one of the least successful visually, old and new elements having been forced together very uncomfortably.

Private Finance Again

The concept of Private Finance Initiatives had first emerged in the mid-1990s, and was originally for projects such as hospitals, prisons and schools. The immediate reward to the contractors lay in the rental payments from the public sector. London Underground had used this Private Finance Initiative framework for projects such as a new ticket issuing and checking system and for devolving power generation to allow the closure of Lots Road power station and rely on the national grid instead.

As described earlier, a significant step forward was taken in 1994 when a suggestion originally made by the rolling stock manufacturer Adtranz was taken up by London Underground. The deal was tendered and the winner was GEC Alstom with a proposal to build 106 6-car trains known as the 1995 stock. The deal saw the private company funding, building and maintaining the trains themselves with London Underground paying a daily service charge for their use; GEC were subject to significant penalties for trains it could not provide to meet the scheduled service, or for failures of trains in service that were found to be its fault. The contractor also assumed responsibility for the depots at Golders Green and Morden. The effect, together with signalling, communications, stations and track in due course moving to the private sector was to remove from London Underground all the short- and long-term engineering decisions. The archaic Treasury practice of allocating capital funds in annual budgets had ensured that London Underground had no assurance that funds would be available to complete a project.

Apart from these structural financial difficulties, the government had, over the course of several years, acquired grave doubts about the ability of London Underground management to handle major projects, with particular reference to the farcical Central Line modernisation scheme, and problems with the Jubilee Line extension to Stratford.

Soon after the Labour government was elected in May 1997 it created an interdepartmental committee to devise a more effective way to invest money in the London Underground. The firm of Price Waterhouse won a consultancy competition and was charged with the task of devising a new, better system. Its report of October 1997 recommended splitting LUL into three groups to look after its infrastructure, and one or more groups to operate the services. A press conference was held on 20th March 1998 at which the Deputy Prime Minister announced the intention to establish a Public-Private Partnership to bring stable, increased investment into London Underground, and to tackle an investment backlog of £2 billion. London Underground would be a

Tube for sale 16p.

Polo. The mint with the hole.

The operation of underground railways in London has rarely been profitable and even in Victorian times railways looked for property and other commercial income to supplement fares revenue, the development of air space over stations being an obvious opportunity. In recent years London Underground has sought to use development opportunities to gain major station improvements at the same time. An example is Fulham Broadway, where there has been an air space development over the platforms, resulting in a new entrance being built, the old entrance being incorporated into the property scheme.

publicly-owned holding company responsible for delivering services, The three privately-owned infrastructure companies (the 'Infracos') would jointly aim to deliver £8 billion of investment in LU over the next 15 years. The contracts would be for a limited period, after which the upgraded assets would revert to the public sector. The successful bidders would be subject to a strict code of service delivery, with fines for failing to deliver all the constituents of the timetabled service and bonus payments for providing an exceptionally good service. The successful bidders (chosen on the basis of value for money in their promises to deliver investment and improvement) had to purchase their franchises from London Underground (£60 million from each member of the Tube Lines consortium, and £75 million from each member of Metronet) but, provided that they fulfilled their side of the bargain, would be able to rely on receiving a regular service charge for up to 30 years.

In July 1998 the Chief Executive of London Transport chaired a conference of industrialists and financiers with the aim of involving prospective investors in the design of the contracts for the PPPs.

By spring 1999 the allocation of lines between the Infracos had become clearer. One obvious grouping was to embrace the sub-surface lines, i.e. the Metropolitan, District, Circle, Hammersmith & City and East London, known collectively as 'SSL'. For the deep-level tube lines two groups were formed, 'BCV' comprising the Bakerloo, Central, Victoria and Waterloo & City, and 'JNP' (known as 'Tube Lines') comprising the Jubilee, Northern and Piccadilly. There was a degree of logic in the tube groupings, including similarities in rolling stock and signalling and in the type of work that needed to be done.

On 18th September 1999 London Underground was divided into the parts which would remain in public ownership (mainly the operational side) and those which would later be taken over by private enterprise but for the time being would remain in the public domain and be tested by 'shadow running'.

The framework with which the bids had to comply was that the franchises should be for a period of 30 years, but that a review of progress, costs and charges would be held after 7½ years, which would give the bidders an opportunity to seek a review of their fees.

Some light relief in the serious business of bidding was introduced by the bizarre intervention of Railtrack, who had expressed interest in the SSL franchise in spring 1999. In the light of the subsequent history of Railtrack it is noteworthy (and a little alarming) that in these early days the government expressed disappointment that Railtrack was not bidding for the deep level tubes as well.

Overnight repairs halt Tube again

By Dick Murray
Transport Editor

TUBE commuters faced delays today when overnight engineering work again failed to finish on time.

Most of the Victoria line was suspended, with only a shuttle service running between King's Cross and Victoria.

Even when the line was reopened there was disruption throughout the morning peak period.

Engineering work on the Victoria line is being carried out by Metronet, the consortium responsible for maintenance over two thirds of the Tube.

The National Audit Office last week raised the problem of night engineering work finishing late — causing 226 morning delays last year.

The first noticeable signs of the takeover of maintenance of the Underground by private companies were a deterioration in morning peak reliability, often caused by engineering work overrunning, and – on a more positive note – improved reliability of signalling and trains. A new programme of station refurbishments got under way, but was well behind schedule according to a March 2005 report to the London Assembly. Track replacement was also below target.

At that time the City of London was being particularly vociferous in demanding a direct rail route between the City and Heathrow Airport. For those using maps as their sole source of information, there appeared to be a quick solution by making a connection from the Heathrow Express line near Paddington to the Hammersmith & City line, and then continuing with trains of main line loading gauge via the Hammersmith & City and Circle lines. The government was so pleased at the possibility of avoiding paying millions of pounds for CrossRail that it gave Railtrack 'preferred bidder' status in the race for the SSL franchise. When the proposal was examined more carefully, however, it was discovered that (i) the Circle platforms were too short for the Heathrow Express type of train, (ii) the Circle Line infrastructure was in other ways unsuitable and (iii) there was no spare line capacity on the northern half of the Circle Line. So, the idea was a non-runner, and Railtrack lost its preferred bidder status in November 1999. In June 2001 it was announced that the PPP contracts were being modified to give greater co-ordination and unification of control. Further modifications were made in October 2001 to strengthen the safety provisions.

The National Audit Office stepped in on 22nd August 2000, saying that it would publish a report in November of that year, which originally would be one month before the preferred bidders were selected. However, this time scale proved to be far too tight for an investigation of such a complex subject, and the NAO returned later.

On 2nd May 2002 the preferred bidders for the two tube PPPs were announced. For the JNP (or Tube Lines) Infraco the winning consortium comprised the firms of Amey, Bechtel-Halcrow and Jarvis. For BCV the winning consortium was Metronet which comprised Balfour Beatty, W. C. Atkins, Thames Water, Seeboard and Bombardier Transportation. Seeboard had been a member of the consortium which had agreed to take over the London Underground power supply by supplying current from the national grid.

Ten days after the announcement of the preferred tube bidders, the National Audit Office began a detailed enquiry into the PPPs, and published its report on 17th June 2004. The enquiry was entitled 'London Underground PPPs – were they good value for money?' The report did not live up to its sweeping title – it was much too early to answer the question, and several years would have to elapse before the value – or otherwise – of the laboriously-constructed and immensely complicated new regime became apparent.

Transport for London, created by the Greater London Authority Act of 1999, was viscerally opposed to the PPP concept, and used every legal procedure to try to halt the whole process. Its political complexion determined that it should oppose any transfer of the publicly-owned London Underground to the private sector. London Underground would not be transferred to TfL until all the PPP deals had been completed. TfL tried to obtain a judicial review but eventually the two sides realised that further argument was useless.

When PPPs were first suggested the fond hope was entertained that the government would no longer have to make up the deficit in London Underground's revenue. However, as the PPPs settled down and the true magnitude of the arrears of maintenance became apparent, this hope was soundly dashed.

The contracts included some relatively severe penalty clauses (called 'abatements', i.e. deductions from the regular Infraco service charge) for failures to provide the foundations of a satisfactory service. These included failure to complete escalator overhaul projects on time, over-runs of overnight engineering works, causing late starts to the service, prolonged station closures; in fact all major delays which were judged to be the fault of the franchisee's team. Any attributable accidents which caused any suspension of services for days on end naturally incurred heavy penalties. On the other side of the coin there were bonuses for good service, but the rate per hour in money was only half the rate for the abatements. The basis of the calculation is a nominal assessment of the value of a passenger's time. The monetary amounts of these payments, although huge in themselves, and especially for reduced availability at busy stations at peak times, were relatively minor in relation to the regular payments made to the franchisees, averaging 1–2% of the payments made by London Underground. Calculating the abatements and bonuses was not merely a simple matter of reading the correct amounts from a table as there was much horse trading involved.

Metronet has had quite a few troubles. On 25th January 2003 a Central Line train derailed at Chancery Lane as a consequence of a traction motor becoming detached. This generated some debate between London Underground and the Infraco (at that point owned by LUL) about maintenance procedures and culminated in the withdrawal of the entire fleet for inspection and subsequent modification. Central Line services

The Thameslink works at Blackfriars included wholesale reconstruction of Blackfriars main line station including major civil engineering works immediately above the District Line platforms. LU took advantage of the situation to modernise its own station. When it reopened on 20th February 2012 it had been entirely transformed.

2012 was a challenging year for the Underground, and, for that matter, other transport in London. First there was the Queen's Diamond Jubilee the main event being held over an extended bank holiday weekend at the beginning of June and which attracted huge number of additional people. Highlights included a 1000-boat parade along the Thames and a huge concert. Then there was the Olympics fortnight beginning at the end of July, having to handle vast number of additional people every day. On some days it was necessary to run last trains up to two hours later than normal to get people home after events at the Olympic stadium at Stratford. Despite widespread forecasts that transport would be a disaster, all went exceedingly well. This was partly a consequence of excellent planning over several years, additional trains operated at times closely tailored to the events (which were spread all over London and not just in one place), a huge management and volunteer presence, and management of Londoner's expectations to encourage reduced ordinary usage at a time when many people are away anyway. A few weeks later the Paralympics followed and went off equally well. During the games period the Underground carried 62 million people, about a third more than normal. The mayor and senior officials may have breathed a sigh of relief, as did many Londoners, proud to have delivered an Olympic Games that went very well. Actually, carrying crowds for major events is something the Underground has a lot of experience of delivering, and it does it well.

Perhaps more of a concern is the everyday traffic of assorted commuters and visitors. The traffic levels are rising faster than the capacity and rising expectations of comfort and value-for-money struggle to be met. A system, much of which was planned (if not actually built) when Queen Victoria was celebrating her own diamond Jubilee, is too small and congested to do much with, at least without huge expense which may better be directed at major cross-London schemes like Crossrail 2 than in continually trying to de-clog some of the existing parts, which is not only expensive but difficult and disruptive. Nevertheless one must at least question just how long it will be possible to manage the deep level tubes so long as they are constrained by 11ft 8¼ins tunnels and as people are getting physically bigger and want to carry large baggage around with them. It is hard to imagine these tunnels lasting another century in this form.

Two Olympic Games travel advisors assist a passenger with her journey.

Above Those with tickets for Olympic events were given a special all zones travelcard. Driving to the games was very much discouraged.

Left Special pink signage appeared in many places to guide people to the Olympic venues.

Steam returns to Baker Street, one of the original stations on the Underground, with Metropolitan loco No. 1 dating from 1898 and built to replace the original No. 1 that had been withdrawn following an accident shortly before.

Our story began with the opening of the Metropolitan – the first Underground railway in the world – in January 1863. It ends with the 150th anniversary celebrations in January 2013. The highlight of these was the operation of a steam train using vintage carriages along the original route on a number of occasions in January 2013. A ballot was held for tickets on two trips open to members of the public, with ticket prices starting at £150. These two trips took place on Sundays 13th and 20th January.

Commemorative coins and stamps were issued the same month. The Royal Mint struck £2 coins with two different designs – one showing the front of a tube train in tunnel and the other showing the roundel. Royal Mail issued ten commemorative stamps, six of which showed different scenes between 1863 and 1999 and four of which each showed three classic Underground posters.

Our detailed coverage of the history of the London Underground ends with its 150th anniversary, but history does not stand still so it is worth recording some of the happenings during the rest of the decade. The main achievement was the total renewal of the trains on the sub-surface lines, whose 150th anniversary was being celebrated. These are the lines that pre-date the deep-level tubes: the Met, the District, Hammersmith & City and Circle lines. For the first time in their history, all of these were now being supplied with a uniform design of train: the S stock. These are impressive trains, with air-conditioning and access to all parts of the passenger areas of the train from inside, the ends of each car being open.

The reverse sides of two designs of £2 coins issued by the Royal Mint.

A display at Farringdon station using the 150th anniversary logo to commemorate posters on the figure 1, significant dates in the Underground's history on the 5 and staff on the zero.

A series of six stamps issued by Royal Mail. A further five showed a selection of poster designs.

2ND

1863

METROPOLITAN RAILWAY OPENS

2ND

1898

TUNNELLING BELOW LONDON STREETS

1ST

1911

COMMUTE FROM THE SUBURBS

1ST

1934

BOSTON MANOR ART DECO STATION

£1.28

1938

CLASSIC ROLLING STOCK

£1.28

1999

JUBILEE LINE AT CANARY WHARF